IN

A

SOLITARY

WAY

MICHELLE LOUISE PIERRE

Copyright © 2018, Michelle Louise Pierre
All rights reserved.

No part of this book *(including the cover photos, which were taken by the author)* may be reproduced, stored in any type of retrieval system, or transmitted by any means, including, but not limited to, electronic, mechanical, photocopying or recording, without written/express permission from the author.

Poems/Commentaries/Prayers contained within this book, were written between the years 1995 and 2018. The cover photo was taken by the author on May 19, 1997, and is entitled, "Shining Alone".

Number Of Poems Included Within, From Author's Other Works, As Follows:
A Consuming Fire (Unpublished) 2
A Pen Of Iron (Unpublished) – 5
Altars Of Praise, Worship, Healing & Deliverance (Unpublished) – 3
As For Me And My House (Unpublished) – 2
Heart Songs Of A Poet (Unpublished) – 3
Speaking In The Light (Unpublished) – 6
The God Of All Comfort (Unpublished) – 6
While I Have My Being (copyright 2002) – 4

The Author's Other Published Works Include:
While I Have My Being – copyright 2002
While I Have My Being, 2nd Edition – copyright 2018

Unless otherwise stated, all Scripture references in this book are taken from the King James Version of the Bible (KJV).

ISBN-13: 978-1-7321274-2-5
ISBN-10: 1732127425

IN DEDICATION

To my LORD and Savior, Jesus Christ, the Messiah, "Thank You!", for Your unfailing faithfulness, unconditional love, and for mercies that are new every morning. God has blessed me with a great many gifts and talents. There is no way that I could ever repay Him for all that He has done for me. Be blessed, oh LORD, by this humble offering of a tithe back to You. To God be the glory!

Further, this book is dedicated in loving memory of:

Louis and Emma Wright, my maternal grandparents, whose love for one another lasted a lifetime. They lived the scriptures by cleaving only to each other, as husband and wife. When my grandfather passed away, I was a very small child. My grandmother, on the other hand, died in 1996, and chose to live out the remainder of her years as a single, Christian woman of high moral character.

Rachel Dixon, or as I called her, "Mother Dixon", went home to be with the LORD, in October of 2005, after being on dialysis for fifteen years *(which is, in and of itself, a miracle directly from the throne of God)*. She was one of the most truly humble and submissive women, I have ever had the pleasure of knowing, and being loved by. Even though she spent the last ten years of her life as a widow, and chose to remain single, she never ceased to be an encouragement to me in my season of singleness. Mother Dixon could get you to chuckle, even in the most dire of circumstances; because, she saw joy, in even the smallest of things. She understood that nothing truly lasts, always, on this side of heaven. She is dearly missed.

Michelle Louise Pierre

ACKNOWLEGEMENTS

I would like to acknowledge my oldest sister, Melva Jean (Pierre) Trask, formerly of New Orleans, Louisiana, *(now of Pine Bluff, Arkansas)*, for being the matriarch in her family structure and pressing on in the face of tremendous, soul numbing, adversity. Thank you, all, in Pine Bluff, for extending your love, in tangible form, to my family, and the countless others, also now residing there from New Orleans, whose lives were completely disrupted in the aftermath of Hurricane Katrina, and the subsequent breaking of the levees which caused loss of lives, property, dignity and, for some, their faith. My prayer is that they have, all, allowed the LORD to be just that in their lives, as He helps them to rebuild. Glory be to God, for some found their faith and/or renewed it, after surviving in the face of the literal storms of life!

I would further like to acknowledge my sister, Melva Jean, because she loved this "little black baby doll", as she called me, from the very first moment she saw me in our mother's arms, after I arrived home for the first time, shortly after her fifth birthday. We all need unconditional love, and her love has blessed my heart tremendously over the years. She and I are also both single, again, and we have shared personal moments together, where we were able to encourage each other's hearts to stay strong and keep on, keeping on. I love you, Big Sis, to the moon, beyond and back!

Secondly, I would like to acknowledge my single, spiritual sisters in Christ, who have walked along this road with me, and have stood the test of time *(each with decades of singleness and friendship)*. Along the way, we have confessed our sins, set-backs, set-ups and disappointments, as well as shared our hearts, joys, tears, hopes, dreams and tons of laughter. Thank you, Evangeline "Vangie" Avila, Barbara Mason and Eirian (Ellis) Williams, whose mother, Felecia Ellis, was another gracious example of a Godly, decades single, mature woman, who lived out her life in a way that blessed my heart, time and time, again *(The fact that she was a total animal lover, was icing on my cake. She never failed to ask how I was doing. Then, how my kitties, Buttons and Coco, were doing, as well. Mom Felecia is surely missed by all of us, she so generously mothered, with that ever present twinkle in her eyes. Who else do you know, would be disappointed when you came for an overnight visit, that you did not bring your kitties along? Smile)*. Girlies, we have certainly been through some stuff – haven't we? Still, in all of that time, we have managed, by the grace of God, to remain friends and confidants as we, all, continue to grow in the LORD and the power of His might! He has truly brought us a mighty long way! Further, I would like say "Thank you" to a more recent single, sister in Christ, Rose Seals, who has been pressing me to "get that book printed", since I first mentioned it to her, last year. Thank you also for just being you, without pretense; and, for being someone I know, who will pray for me at the drop of a hat. I love you, all!

Lastly, I would surely be remiss, if I did not acknowledge, as my way of saying "Thank you!" to all of you, who tangibly demonstrated your support for my ministry in psalms by purchasing my first book, <u>While I Have My Being</u>, as well as for those, who subsequently purchased the updated version of that book, <u>While I Have My Being – 2nd Edition</u>. I would also like to express my gratitude to those of you, whom I know I can count on to read the poems, and commentaries, I send out through the e-mail, text, or status messages on social media, who will take few moments, out of your busy schedules, to send me an encouraging reply.

March 27, 2018 – Tuesday – 1:02 am

Michelle Louise Pierre

CONTENTS

Dedication		iii
Acknowledgments		v
Introduction		xiii
Foreword		xv
SCCRIPTURAL THEME – Psalm 107: 1 – 9		xvii
The Poet Sings, Again…		1
In A Solitary Way		3
A Child Of God	*(From – The God Of All Comfort)*	4
A Clean Heart		6
A Consecration		7
A Prayer of Solitude		8
A Restless Heart		9
A Servant's Heart	*(From – The God Of All Comfort)*	10
A Soul's Expression		13
An Unmarried Woman		14
An Unwed Wife		16
Are You Free?	*(From – A Pen Of Iron)*	17
At First Glance	*(From – A Pen Of Iron)*	18
Baptism By Fire!	*(From – A Consuming Fire)*	19
Before		21
Bless Him, Today	*(From – The God Of All Comfort)*	22
Bless My Husband		23
Celibacy's Song		24
Come Correct, Or Don't Get Dressed!	*(From – A Pen Of Iron)*	25
Conversations With Grace		26

Counterfeit Love		28
Dare I…		29
Dating In The Dark	*(From – A Pen Of Iron)*	30
Dear Lord, The Man		33
Deep Calleth Unto Deep	*(From – The God Of All Comfort)*	34
Divine Protection		35
Enough!		37
Father, Is He The One?		39
For, This Is The Will Of God		40
Freeing You, To Love	*(From – Heart Songs Of A Poet)*	41
Get Back Up!	*(From – The God Of All Comfort)*	43
God Said, "No", Again!		46
Happy Valentine's Day		47
Heart Of My Heart	*(From – Heart Songs Of A Poet)*	48
Hello, Self!	*(From – While I Have My Being)*	49
I Am A Wall	*(From – Heart Songs Of A Poet)*	51
I Am Looking For Jesus		52
I Can Feel Your Heart		53
I Fell In Love, Today, Again		54
I Have Learned Some Things		55
I Miss You, Already		57
I Press	*(From – While I Have My Being)*	58
I Promised Him		60
I See You & I See You, Too		61
I Will Fall Into Your Heart		63
I Will Need You		64

If We Had Not Believed!		65
In A Single Moment		66
In Love, Alone?		67
In The Light Of Day		68
Integrity	*(From – Speaking In The Light)*	69
Intimacy Without Touch		70
Into Your Arms		71
It's Okay To Love, Again		72
Just Between Us		74
Just The Touch		75
Knit Together By God		76
Little Girl, I Love You	*(From – The God Of All Comfort)*	77
Living Single, Gloriously!		80
Lord, At What Price This Blessing?		81
Love, From Your Valentine's Heart		83
Mere Words		84
My Strength, My Song, My Salvation		85
My Valentine's Heart		86
Never Any Slack		87
Night Song		88
No Matter What It Looks Like		89
No Man Enough For Me		90
Not Without Jesus!		91
One Plus One Equals One	*(From – Speaking In The Light)*	92
Only The Lord!		95
Opened My Heart To Love, Again		96

Peeping Through The Gate	*(From – A Pen Of Iron)*	97
Pray For Me		99
Predestined Love!		101
Prodigal Daughter		102
Ready To Be In Love		104
Renew Our Strength		105
Rest In Hope		106
Shattered!	*(From – Altars of Praise, Worship, Healing & Deliverance)*	107
Single and Satisfied		110
Single Glory		111
Single Praise!		112
Single Valentine		113
Single Valentine's Heart		114
Singleness Of Heart		115
Singly Graced and Abundantly Blessed		116
So, This Is Unconditional Love?		117
Solitude	*(From – Altars of Praise, Worship, Healing & Deliverance)*	119
Stay Open And Honest	*(From – While I Have My Being)*	121
Steppin' Into The New		122
The Bond Of Your Love		124
The Box		125
The Crush Of Loneliness		127
The Door Of Your Heart		128
The Gate	*(From – Speaking In The Light)*	129
The Healing Season		132
The Land Of Regret		133

The Measure Of Faith		134
The Offering	*(From – Altars of Praise, Worship, Healing & Deliverance)*	135
The Onion	*(From – Speaking In The Light)*	137
The Voice Of My Beloved		140
Too Blessed To Be Depressed	*(From – While I Have My Being)*	141
Unfulfilled Life	*(From – Speaking In The Light)*	142
What Do People See?	*(From – Speaking In The Light)*	146
When An Intercessor Weeps	*(From – A Consuming Fire)*	148
When Faith Meets The Fire!	*(From – As For Me And My House)*	149
When I Met Jesus, For The First Time		150
Who Is On The Lord's Side?		152
With The Entrance Of Each New Dawn		154
Within…		155
Without A Doubt		156
Written In Heaven		157
Yet, Again		159
Yield!	*(From – As For Me And My House)*	161
Yield To His Praise		163
You Have Blessed My Heart		165
Your Will, Your Way		166

A TIME OF REASONING   168

Isaiah 1: 18 & 19	169
A Good Thing	170
A Song	174
If Thine Eye Be Single	175
Just Don't Let It Touch Me!	177

Me, Can Do It!	179
Step By Step	180
Psalm 51 & On-Going Prayer Requests	182
IN CONCLUSION OF THIS MATTER	185
Conclusion – 2006	186
An Uncoupled Soul, In The Midst Of Mourning	187
Conclusion – 2018	189
About The Author	191
CLOSING SCRIPTURE – Psalm 68: 1 – 6a	192
Notes and/or Insights	193

INTRODUCTION

This book, <u>In A Solitary Way</u>, is not just a book of poetry. It is also includes commentary, from the time when I, too, walked in a solitary way. Several of these poems are also located in other books, but there are also ones that were exclusively written just for this publication. The idea for this book was given to me by the Lord, many moons ago, but it was not until I started facilitating workshops geared towards single women, that I began "pulling poems" from various other books to form packets that I could hand out to them. However, the idea really jelled into place on April 21, 2002, when I was blessed with the opportunity (at the invitation of their singles leaders, Reverends Wayne and Cynthia Jackson) to stand before a group of single adults at Fremont Bible Fellowship in Fremont, California and read some of the poems that I selected for the occasion. When I shared with them that I was also writing a book that would contain poems geared towards single adults, the response I received from them, told me that it was one that was long overdue. That is when I seriously began to get down to the business of formulating this book. As in most of my other books, I wanted this one to also contain seventy-seven poems. Since, I was nowhere near having that amount, serious prayer had to be focused on the task. Thank You, Lord, for pouring through me the lines and verses necessary to bring this project to fruition. I thank You, in advance, this Saturday, May 18, 2002, for this work that will be a reflection of Your glory as it flows through pen and keyboard out to the singles-in-waiting. May these poems bless Your heart, oh Lord! Amen.   May 18, 2002   Saturday – 12:28 PM

… Wow, a lot has happened since I wrote the paragraph above as the introduction to this book. At the time, I wrote it, I was in the process of putting the finishing touches on another book of poetry called, <u>While I Have My Being</u>, which was inspired by Psalm 104:33, *"I will sing unto the LORD as long as I live: I will sing praise to my God while I have my being"*. It was self-published in 2002 and came out in August of that same year.

I have chosen to leave the "original introduction" along with this introduction, because I felt that it stays true to the creative process. It is like beginning a painting, with a chosen palate of colors in hand, only to begin the work and find that more mixing needs to take place, to get just the right affect. Then, when all is said and done "your masterpiece" is there in front of you. And, to be completely honest, more often than not, it looks nothing like what you originally envisioned. It is in those times, for me, as a Christian artist, that I know the LORD is the driving force behind that work; and, I am most grateful that He, for that time in space, has chosen me to work through.

As you can tell by the time span between the date of the original "Introduction" and this one, it has actually been over four and a half years, since I first began to compile these poems. As you can see, the final work now contains one hundred and four poems, spanning slightly over eleven years – October 5, 1995 with "Shattered" to October 27, 2006 with "When I Met Jesus, For The First Time". There is also a section in the back called, "A Time Of Reasoning", where I have chosen to include five commentaries, for reflection. Out of the one hundred and four poems included, only twenty nine can also be found scattered within the pages of a few of my other works. They have been noted accordingly. One of the poems, "God Said, "No", Again!" is actually a continuation of one I included in my previously published work, <u>While I Have My Being</u> *(1st and 2nd Editions)*, entitled, "God Said, "No!" The creation of that 2nd edition is quite another story in, and of, itself *(published March, 2018 – Thank You, LORD!!!)*.

Over the last four and a half years, a great deal has happened in my life. But, through it all, I have been writing, writing and writing. The LORD, in His sovereign grace and mercy, has patiently and faithfully walked with me through one thing after another, in this my season of singleness. Still, I must note that, not all of the experiences related to in these writings, have been mine, personally. Some were gleaned from things I have seen or heard; and, as I thought on them, I felt they were being pushed through my soul, by the LORD, as an additional way to minister to someone else's needs. Now, I feel that the LORD is telling me, it is the time to have this body of work published. I had to smile, to myself, when I read the "original introduction" and discovered that the church I spoke about, at that time, had down the line become my home church. In that time period, they moved locations from Fremont to Newark, so it is now called, Family Bible Fellowship *(still FBF)*, under the same leadership, Pastor Horacio S. Jones and First Lady, Florence V. Jones. It never ceases to amaze me how the LORD puts you right where you need to be, to do the work that He has called you to do. We certainly do serve an awesome God, who then, in my case, moves you on, when He deems it is time to do so. At the present time, I am a member of New Hope Christian Fellowship Church in Hayward, CA. My senior pastors are Timothy Russell and Victor Cervantes, who are godly men, with wives, Vanessa and Cindee, respectively, who also love and serve the LORD.

Due to the fact that I will be married, again, one day, "if the LORD tarries" as the older saints used to say, most of the poems, which poured out of my heart, are geared towards those, whom like myself, have been single for years and are actively in the process of waiting, which to us, can at times seem like a contradiction in terms. Because, how does one "actively wait" *(smile)*? More importantly than that, my heart's desire is that you will see, and be moved by, the power of the LORD to transform, through the accepted, free gift of salvation and the acknowledged need for repentance, a solitary soul, who has not always been willing to be transformed; and, still has a moment, now and again, where this is the case, like stated in Ephesians 1:1-10. Thank You, LORD, for love, grace, mercy, healing, forgiveness and deliverance!

My prayer for this completed work of art is that you will be touched by the LORD, in whatever manner He has determined necessary, to draw you closer to His Son, Jesus Christ. I pray that you will be able to personally relate to something contained within these pages, and that it will spark a light of remembrance in your own solitary soul. In doing so, I hope it will bring laughter, a smile, a tear, a blush, or just a plain old "ouch". Those are just a few of the things, I have encountered, in this project's reading and writing process. So, come along on this path that is lain before you, and see what the LORD has chosen for you, in this time and this season.

Looking back on these words in this year, 2018, as I ready this work, finally, for publication, I cannot help but to be amazed by the difference between God's timing and, in this case, mine. I bow to You, oh LORD, and say in humble submission, with my heart's cry, "Thy will be done!" Thank You, LORD!!!

October 28, 2006   Saturday – 1:00 PM   *Updated: March 12, 2018   Monday – 2:32 am*

…Obviously, with all of my good intentions, this work was put on the back burner, yet again; but, this time for several months, not years. However, during that time, several more poems have been added, bringing the total up to one hundred and seventeen! Out of that total, thirty-one are included in additional works. In the section entitled, <u>A Time Of Reasoning</u>, a new commentary, coupled with a prayer, called, "Step By Step" was also added. In the final section, <u>In Conclusion Of This Matter,</u> a commentary entitled, "An Uncoupled Soul, In The Midst of Mourning", was then added, and will explain why this last delay took place. Further, at closing, "On-Going Prayer Requests", using Psalm 51, for inspiration, was added, as well. God, as always, is in the midst, and He, obviously, wanted the additional poems, the prayer, scriptures, and the commentaries included in this work *(the last poem was actually written this past Sunday, 7.29.18)*. After all, the LORD definitely knows best! To God be the glory, both, now and forever!!! Hallelujah and Amen!!!

In His Love, Service and Devotion,
Michelle Louise Pierre
Final Update: July 11, 2018 – Wednesday – 8:17 pm to July 31, 2018 – Tuesday – 11:45 pm

21stcenturypsalmist@gmail.com
www.21stcenturypsalmist.com

FOREWORD

When Ms. Pierre asked me to write this foreword, I was honored and excited. This book is written to both single men and women. I know this group of privileged individuals because I am one of them. In a room full of people, there is an unspoken language, a sigh of hope, great expectation, some desperation and contentment in each of our eyes. The deepest expression of a man's soul is from his heart.

In A Solitary Way is written from the heart. There are many intellectual books written to singles who have never married, widowed or divorced, but none of them have quite captured the gist of where we really live. Don't get me wrong, there has been good advice and Godly wisdom, but few have the courage to speak of the struggle that exists, to come to a place of authenticity within yourself and their relationship with the Lord, and be able to share both their deepest thoughts and feelings.

There were times when reading **In A Solitary Way** that I felt like I was imposing on intimate sessions with Ms. Pierre, and the Lord, and being exposed all at the same time. The silent war I once struggled, is no longer; there are others who have felt as I. I challenge you to take the journey through this book of poetry, ask the Holy Spirit to be your guide, work through some buried emotions, and open up a deeper part of yourself. You will be challenged and you will make new discoveries about yourself. These discoveries will deepen your connection with others and the Lord.

Valerie Doyle, MA (Written in 2006)

Psalm 107: 1 – 9

O give thanks unto the LORD, for he is good: for his mercy endureth for ever. Let the redeemed of the LORD say so, whom he hath redeemed from the hand of the enemy; And gathered them out of the lands, from the east, and from the west, from the north, and from the south. They wandered in the wilderness in a solitary way; they found no city to dwell in. Hungry and thirsty, their soul fainted in them. Then they cried unto the LORD in their trouble, and he delivered them out of their distresses. And he led them forth by the right way, that they might go to a city of habitation. Oh that men would praise the LORD for his goodness, and for his wonderful works to the children of men! For he satisfieth the longing soul, and filleth the hungry soul with goodness.

THE POET SINGS, AGAIN...

Michelle Louise Pierre

IN A SOLITARY WAY

Chasing
What
The
LORD
Is
Saying
To
Me
Through
Rhyme

One
Word
Carefully
Given
In
Metered
Time

Wanting
To
Go
In
A
Solitary
Way
Gently
Led
In
Another

The
Holy
Ghost
Is
Directing
Conducting
Orchestrating
Like
No
Other

March 2, 2001 – Friday

A CHILD OF GOD

Psalm 42: 1 & 2
As the hart panteth after the water brooks,
so panteth my soul after thee, O God.
My soul thirsteth for God, for the living God:
when shall I come and appear before God?

Hunger and thirst in the soul that only God can fill
Allowing only Him access to your innermost parts
Desiring the Word of the Lord above all else

Seeking to please Him in thought, word and deed
Needing to be near Him to feel His touch
A touch that sustains your very life

Imparting wisdom, drunk in
From the everlasting fountain of eternal life
Flowing in this life and the next

The living water that never runs dry
The well that contains sustenance
To preserve your soul from death

Loving Him intimately, one on one
Hoping above all else to be counted
Amongst the righteous upon His return

Knowing His return is eminent
Seeking His face in the clouds
With joyful anticipation, not dread

Yet, getting down to the business
Of living your life to the fullest
While still on this earth

Holding on to your integrity
Not compromising your morals, to fit in
When caught up in sin, sincerely repenting
Attitude of humble submission and contrition

Allowing His love to comfort your troubled heart
Accepting His outstretched hand
In all of the many forms that it will come

In A Solitary Way

Using prayer, praise and worship as fuel
Keeps you going throughout the day
Acknowledge Christ as Savior and Lord
Even in the face of persecution, ridicule

Willing to die for your beliefs
Understanding that earthly death
Is just a path to eternity with God

Covering yourself, daily, in the blood of Jesus
Fearing no man, the enemy or the world
Fearing only in reverential respect, love and honor
The God of your salvation

Knowing with all certainty
Without a shadow of a doubt
With the clarity of a mindset totally free

That You Belong To The Lord
That You Are, Most Definitely, His Child

Amen!!!

October 18, 1996 – Friday
(From The Book: The God Of All Comfort)

A CLEAN HEART

Psalm 51: 10 – 12
Create in me a clean heart, O God; and renew a right spirit within me.
Cast me not away from thy presence; and take not thy holy spirit from me.
Restore unto me the joy of thy salvation; and uphold me with thy free spirit.

Romans 3: 23 – 25
For all have sinned, and come short of the glory of God; Being justified freely by
his grace through the redemption that is in Christ Jesus: Whom God hath set forth
to be a propitiation through faith in his blood, to declare his righteousness for
the remission of sins that are past, through the forbearance of God.

There have been times, over the years, in all honesty,
some not so distant, as a single, Christian adult, that I have
found myself embroiled in rebellion and sin, so great in my
estimation, that I felt entombed by shame, hurt, anger and doubt.
At those times, I have cried bucket loads of tears, when
true repentance hit; but, before that, I merely made excuses
for my shameless behavior, not really wanting to let go of the
enticements of sin, or have it from my heart, in anyway, put out.

Thank You, LORD, for being the revealer of all things done in the cloying,
obscurity of darkness that must be brought under the scrutiny of Your
precious light; for, it is those times, that the false pleasure of those moments,
grow strangely dim, as Your pull on my soul, did not let go of my heart.
Thank You, for persevering with this wild, unruly child, at times, when
being disobedient really meant nothing to me, because according the
corrupt world view, I felt that being in total control of my own life,
was the best, firmly handled, in all situations, right from the start.

• • • • •

Thank You, for the cleansing rain that has washed the dross out of our
lives and our souls, to the extent that we can remain humble, with the
ultimate desire, living in our hearts, to cross the finish line in this most
holy race; and, when our time comes, hear, "Well done…" from You.
Dear LORD, thank You for the blessed belief in the Holy Trinity that
molds and shapes us into the people, You formed in our mothers' wombs,
who once forgiven and cleansed in grace with unmerited favor, would then
be generously enfolded in Your loving hands of mercy, all of lives through.

April 26, 2018 – Thursday

In A Solitary Way

A CONSECRATION

Romans 12: 1 – 3
I beseech you therefore, brethren, by the mercies of God, that ye present your bodies a living sacrifice, holy, acceptable unto God, which is your reasonable service. And be not conformed to this world: but be ye transformed by the renewing of your mind, that ye may prove what is that good, and acceptable, and perfect, will of God. For I say, through the grace given unto me, to every man that is among you, not to think of himself more highly than he ought to think; but to think soberly, according as God hath dealt to every man the measure of faith.

I want all that You, Dear LORD, have for me.
I will not shrink back from my divine destiny.
Worldly lures and blinding sin, I must flee.
I covenant with You, oh LORD, in submission to Thee.

My heart is being tested right now, to see if I will stand.
To stay the course You laid before me, the one You planned.
Not running off foolishly, leaving this temple unmanned.
I must keep my trust completely in You, not in me or any man.

The pull of another chance at human love is very strong.
Still, I must stay prayerful, not letting flesh pull me along.
I must feed my spirit, trusting in You, not to lead me wrong.
For I can truly have You, both, if I don't forget my heavenly song.

The song You gave me in the still of those dark, lonely nights.
The song that chased those shadows from my heart, with Your light.
The song that tramples upon doubt, telling me it will be all right.
The song, inspired by the Holy Ghost, in the power of Your might.

LORD, sure me up in this time of weakness, make my pathway clear.
I will press into Your love, listening to no other, Your voice I must hear.
Once heard, give me the courage to proceed, draw me near.
Dear LORD, in this place where the rubber meets the road, help me not to veer.

Knowing full well, left to my own devises, I can certainly do no good thing.
My righteousness is from You, and to You, I must desperately cling.
Don't let me be sidetracked by this man, bearing a potential wedding ring.
You have kept me all of these years, alone with You, giving me that song to sing.

I am royalty, for You have preordained it to be so, a member of Your holy nation.
Sure up my soul; for Your love, everlasting, is given freely without hesitation.
Strengthen me, Holy Ghost, to win this battle, I must not forget my final destination.
Cover me in Your Son's blood as I begin this time of prayer, fasting and consecration.

August 12, 2002 – Monday

Michelle Louise Pierre

A PRAYER IN SOLITUDE

Matthew 6: 6
But thou, when thou prayest, enter into thy closet, and when
thou hast shut thy door, pray to thy Father which is in secret;
and thy Father which seeth in secret shall reward thee openly.

Dear LORD, thank You for the blessings of this day that have come and
the peaceful, joy that You have given, to extend grace to those I see.
Now, back in my own space where thoughts of You can be given
the time they need to formulate and pour forth from me.

LORD, I am so grateful, as Your warmth spreads from the top of my
head downward, marinating me in the anointing oil of Your sweet embrace.
Tears perch on my eyelids as I am overwhelmed by all of the sweet rescues
made on my behalf, as You have extended to me, over and over, again, Your grace.

The Holy Spirit is taking me to a place where I have not been in a long time, a place
of intimate fellowship, especially designed by Your loving hand, for this time and place.
Heavenly Father, I want to run out of here, yet curl up into a ball at the same time,
to just let Your love totally envelop me, in Your sweet, all consuming, holy embrace.

As praises rise out of my belly, like steam from a kettle set upon on a hot flame,
they tumble out on this page, not wanting our intimate time together to end.
LORD, may I never tire of Your touch and heed all Your intimate calls, where
I can be encapsulated in the unconditional love of Jesus, my Savior and friend.

Heavenly Father, blessed be Jesus' holy name; for, my heart's prayer is
that the fruit of my life brings You glory, for everything that You have done.
May You receive the glory and honor You are due, if for nothing else,
than for the monumental, sacrificial love it took to give to us, all, Your Son.

October 23, 2006 – Monday

In A Solitary Way

A RESTLESS HEART

A restless heart
knows no loyalties.
It cares not for how things
should, or used to, be.

It only cares that it feels
lonely and wants relief.
Knowing that pursuing that outside
of God's will, will bring grief.

A restless heart hungers for
the things that will give it rest.
Following the ways of the world,
that at the moment, seem best.

It has tired of waiting for the
promises of the Lord, to be fulfilled.
Its only goal, now, is to settle down into
the love, life has to offer, and be stilled.

A restless heart will take you to
places where you should not go.
It will convince you that in so doing, it can
be hidden, no one would have to know.

It will take you ever so subtly away,
from seeking after the heart of God.
Leading you into uncharted pastures,
away from the Lord's protective rod.

Dear Lord, in my soul, I desire
to live a life of purity and holiness.
Calm the restlessness in my heart,
relieve the tension and the stress.

Cleanse me of my secret faults, forgive me,
Lord, this is, now, my restful heart's desire.
Thank You, for filling it with Your love and the
desire to worship You, with a newly kindled fire.

In Jesus' holy and righteous name, I pray. Amen!

November 1, 2003 – Saturday

Michelle Louise Pierre

A SERVANT'S HEART

Exodus 33: 13 & 14
Now therefore, I pray thee, if I have found grace
in thy sight, show me now thy way, that I may know thee,
that I may find grace in thy sight: and consider that this
nation is thy people. And he said, My presence
shall go with thee, and I will give thee rest.

Kneeling down beside your bed to pray
Feeling His love tug on the strings of your heart
Pray for this one and that one, the Lord says
You obey

You are no longer your own
You were bought with a price
A debt that you could not surely pay, on your own

What is your reasonable service?
Is it 9 to 5 or some such thing?
More like, 24 and 7

Remembering a time when
You were not so compliant
In fact, You were downright defiant

You bumped your head a lot
Had to rub and soothe a great many sore spots
Yet, you, through His miraculous grace
Have learned a great many things
Not the least of which has been obedience

This obedience
Not nurtured from a place of fear and trepidation
Nurtured from the loving bosom of your Savior, Jesus
Nurtured from the place of healing, love and forgiveness
Nurtured by realizing that He desires only your best

Desiring only that which is in your best interest
Anything less, is unacceptable, detrimental
You are much too valuable in His sight

Sweet peace and rest, at last
Found at the hand of total, complete surrender
Surrendering to the only One, who can, and has, restored

In A Solitary Way

Taking a fragmented, shattered soul
Loving the pieces back together, making you whole

It's time to serve others from that same nourishing plate
The contents of which have sustained your hungry soul

This is too good to keep to yourself
He did not bring you through all that, to sit

Feet moving forward, marching to His beat
He energizes like no other can
You reach out your hand to others
Strengthened by His hand at your back

When weariness comes
You have had to learn to lean even more fully on Him
He is teaching you to help, then walk away
Off to the next assignment

The flesh wants recognition, praise
The Spirit says, "Wait"
Learning that your rewards only matter
When they are from the Master's hand

This has been a tough lesson to learn
But, one that has brought immeasurable peace
A peace that enlivens the very core of your existence
Filling in the areas formerly reserved for someone else

Reserved for something else that was always
Just outside of your reach
At times, so desperate in the reaching, that you have slipped
Fallen actually, a time or two, leading to utter chaos

Now peace has become a very precious commodity
You ask for His wisdom daily
You are learning to accept His wise counsel

In the spirit of repentance, humility
Allowing Him to put you in a place of rest

A place where you can truly hear
What He has been trying to say
Where visions can freely flow again

Tears stream down your face
Feeling His undying love afresh

Michelle Louise Pierre

Renewal sweeps through your soul
Replenished, revived
Coddled, loved, chastised and set back aright

. . . . .

It's time for you to get back on the battlefield

The field where the harvest is ripe

The field where the King of kings reigns supreme

The field where He once found you, face down

The field where you have been sent back to, in love, serve

Matthew 9: 35 – 38
And Jesus went about all the cities and villages, teaching in their synagogues, and preaching the gospel of the kingdom, and healing every sickness and every disease among the people. But when he saw the multitudes, he was moved with compassion on them, because they fainted, and were scattered abroad, as sheep having no shepherd. Then saith he unto his disciples, The harvest truly is plenteous, but the labourers are few; Pray ye therefore the Lord of the harvest, that he will send forth labourers into his harvest.

January 14, 1997 – Tuesday
(From the Book – The God Of All Comfort)

A SOUL'S EXPRESSION

I woke up this morning with these words running through my head,
and a peace in my heart that is still resting sweetly here within me.
I wish that I was there, with you now, sitting next to you, with my
head on your strong shoulder, as we will surely one day be.

I believe in you, Honey, for I sensed in my spirit, sometime ago,
that you would hold a very special place in my heart.
With every line you wrote to me, I felt the ice sickles around me
begin to melt in sweet surrender, which gave me a start.

I sensed our life would be one filled with a joy and happiness that neither of us
could have imagined, when we were going through our separate times of trial.
Still, the matrimonial road would not always be smooth before us, but the
LORD promised to tame our solitary hearts that had previously run wild.

Not tamed to the place where passion would no longer exist,
and our lives together would become routine and humdrum.
For there is a passion for life between us that was birthed in our spirits
before we were born, for which Jesus' blood paid for all, not just some.

LORD, continue to order our steps, guiding us by the Holy Spirit
into those areas of wisdom, tempered with understanding, divine.
Let the knowledge we need to succeed in ministry to each other, and those
whom You bring into our lives, go beyond these vessels You have refined.

Help us to walk circumspectly before You, oh LORD, with You, daily, teaching
us how in submission, to humble our hearts to one another, second only to You.
Help us to know how to operate in the Spirit, in all areas of our lives, recognizing
the enemy's ploys, so that we may with each attack, victoriously come through.

Dear LORD, as long as we live we will never be able to fully express
our gratitude to You, for making us a part of each other's divine destiny.
Continue to cover us under the protective shield of Your omnipotent love,
building within us a loving trust for one another, filled with Your majesty.

October 21, 2006 – Saturday

Michelle Louise Pierre

AN UNMARRIED WOMAN

1 Corinthians 7: 32 - 34
But I would have you without carefulness. He that is unmarried careth for the things that belong to the Lord, how he may please the Lord: But he that is married careth for the things that are of the world, how he may please his wife. There is difference also between a wife and a virgin. The unmarried woman careth for the things of the Lord, that she may be holy both in body and in spirit: but she that is married careth for the things of the world, how she may please her husband.

This is not a new message,
but one that has just completely
taken root in the depths of my soul.
I am an unmarried woman, after all,
and I have to remind myself, daily,
to give You, my Lord full control.

You have truly brought me from a mighty
long way, since that time when I was so young,
and in a marriage destined for divorce.
You swooped in, hearing my delirious ravings,
taking a spirit that was so broken, placing me
lovingly back on the right course.

Hallelujah, bless the Lord, for without, You,
I would not have been able to pick myself
back up, after that descent into hell.
I was so wounded, there were times when
I could not even utter a sound aloud, but
You, Dear Lord, heard my soul yell.

It screamed from a place deep inside, causing me
to answer a knock on the door of my heart,
that had been going on for years.
I, in my desperate loneliness and bitterness
of heart, could never truly have heard
that knock, over the sound of my silent tears.

Thank You, Lord, for ministering to my
heart then, when I had no hope of a
future, that would be this bright.
Thank You, for stepping into that snapshot
of my life, dispelling the haunting, accusing
darkness with Your holy, healing light.

In A Solitary Way

You have given me, opportunity upon opportunity
since that time, those years long past, to minister
Your love to other desperately lonely hearts.
Lord, thank You, for each time You used me to
step in, on time, to tell another living soul, that from
that life of sadness and despair, they could also depart.

Lord, my mind, of late has been focusing on making
wedding plans and arrangements that have taken
my focus, little by little, away from You.
I have found myself at times, being completely
confused in thought as to what next step
I should take, let alone what I should do.

Lord, thank You, for speaking through the heart
of Pastor Dace, yesterday morning as he ministered
to the souls of the married and singles in the house.
In so doing, I have come to realize that until
I am actually married, I owe my allegiance completely
to You, for You are my first love, and my spouse.

Continue to teach me how to be the wife and
woman, whom You created me to be before
I was even a blip on life's ever evolving screen.
Accept the repentance in my heart, set me back
aright, as off of that arm of flesh, I was trying to
depend upon, I turn back to, upon You, solidly lean.

February 9, 2004 – Monday

Michelle Louise Pierre

AN UNWED WIFE

Dear LORD, I want to be married so badly,
sometimes the desire seems to overwhelm my
heart, cutting through me, sharp as a knife.
I am growing weary of going to wedding after
wedding, being in wedding after wedding, wondering
when the day will come for me to be someone's wife.

When will I make a presentation before the family
and friends, in a beautiful gown, with a veil
covering my face, as I walk down that church aisle.
I long for a time when that will be me and at the end
of that walk awaits the man, whom I have given my
heart too, standing there with a great, big loving smile.

Divorced friends speak about how devastating it was,
without knowing that I am a little envious, because at
least they have had a turn up to the matrimonial plate.
Still, knowing them as I do, they were hurt right
down to the core, when it all fell apart, and saving
their marriage seemed to come a day way too late.

Either way, LORD, I, just for this moment, want
to concentrate on what is now going on inside of
my own head, tapping into it, exposing it, being real.
I do want to be married, one day soon, but I know in
my heart of hearts, that without You putting us together,
I will choose not to be married, without You holy seal.

One day that choice seems to come easily, still on
other days is seems to come out like little drips of water
in a clogged pipe, headed straight down the drain.
Strengthen me, oh LORD, to await the fulfillment of my
heart's desire, and for that, I must learn to continuously
submit to You, giving You total, complete reign.

October 26, 2006 – Thursday

In A Solitary Way

<u>ARE YOU, FREE?</u>

You say, you want a husband
and you say, you want a wife.
When, what you bring to the table
is nothing but a plate full of strife.

You have emotional baggage hanging off of
both shoulders and your hands are full, too.
What in the world would anybody in
their right, sanctified mind, want with you?

Go back to the fountain and drink
from the water that never runs dry.
Dear One, only the blood of our sweet,
Savior Jesus can cleanse you, deep on the inside.

This type of deep healing is not going to come in the
form of a woman, a man, or even a worldly type drink.
In fact, it is going to come in the form of something that in
your confused state, right now, you cannot even imagine or think.

But, rest assured for it will be found by staying in His Presence
and humbly allowing that deep healing and purging to begin.
Get alone with the Master, and don't look for a mate,
right now, when the best you can handle is a friend.

I don't mean any harm, for certainly, we all
need help from time to time, but facts are still facts.
Seek deliverance and hand your burdens over to the Lord,
as He fills you with His Spirit, like in the Book of Acts.

Then, once healed and delivered, the veil will be removed
from your eyes, so that you will be able to use wisdom to see.
But, right now, Dear Heart, put the transmission into reverse,
and squarely answer the question, for yourself,

"Are You, Really, Free?"

August 19, 1999 – Thursday
(From The Book – A Pen Of Iron)

Michelle Louise Pierre

AT FIRST GLANCE

In love, in that first glance
Lord, I won't miss my last chance

He nodded his head and smiled my way
My heart began to wildly flutter, then sway

He's coming over, now, Bible firmly in hand
The closer he gets, I start making wedding plans

Mrs. So and So, I've waited all of my life
I just know, I'll make him a wonderful wife

Even closer, now, and I can tell that he will be my perfect mate
Every hair is in place, and in that suit, he looks so great

Face to face, now, I smile and say, God bless you, in greeting, adding an amen
The Lord had moved that Sunday, but his reply was that he wanted to be my friend

He complimented me on my hair, my face, my eyes and even my manner of dress
He said that he had looked around the whole church, and, to him, I looked the best

As I stood there in the after-glow, basking in the Lord's Presence, that on my face, did show
I took another look at that man, with that fleshly look in his eyes, we have all come to know

Dear Lord, I thanked him, then politely stepped aside as I continued to prepare to go home
He, momentarily stunned, shrugged, took aim on someone else and continued his roam

I reached my car, drove off, came in my front door and started a thanksgiving dance
Dear Father, thank You, for teaching me to look a lot further and deeper, than at first glance

JUDE 12 & 17 - 19
*These are spots in your feasts of charity, when they feast with you, feeding
themselves without fear: clouds they are without water, carried about of winds;
trees whose fruit withereth, without fruit, twice dead, plucked up by the roots;...
But, beloved, remember ye the words which were spoken before of the apostles
of our Lord Jesus Christ; How that they told you there should be mockers in
the last time, who should walk after their own ungodly lusts. These be
they who separate themselves, sensual, having not the Spirit.*

June 1, 1999 – Tuesday
(From The Book – A Pen Of Iron)

BAPTISM OF FIRE!

Isaiah 6: 1 – 8
In the year that king Uzziah died I saw also the Lord sitting upon a throne, high and lifted up, and his train filled the temple. Above it stood the seraphims: each one had six wings; with twain he covered his face, and with twain he covered his feet, and with twain he did fly. And one cried unto another, and said, Holy, holy, holy, is the LORD of hosts: the whole earth is full of his glory. And the posts of the door moved at the voice of him that cried, and the house was filled with smoke. Then said I, Woe is me! for I am undone; because I am a man of unclean lips, and I dwell in the midst of a people of unclean lips: for mine eyes have seen the King, the LORD of hosts. Then flew one of the seraphims unto me, having a live coal in his hand, which he had taken with the tongs from off the altar: And he laid it upon my mouth, and said, Lo, this hath touched thy lips; and thine iniquity is taken away, and thy sin purged. Also I heard the voice of the Lord, saying, Whom shall I send, and who will go for us?
Then said I, Here am I; send me.

Luke 3: 15 & 16
And as the people were in expectation, and all men mused in their hearts of John, whether he were the Christ, or not; John answered, saying unto them all, I indeed baptize you with water; but one mightier than I cometh, the latchet of whose shoes I am not worthy to unloose: he shall baptize you with the Holy Ghost and with fire

I woke up this morning having a conversation with the LORD,
about a question on my heart that has been there for quite some time,
as it laid dormant, it simmers, then percolates, before it fully forms.
I could not fathom why people, who have served the LORD for many
years, still seemed so anemic; while, appearing to unquestionably accept
defeat and bondage, as they crumble so easily in the face of life storms.

Dear LORD, that's when You began to speak to me about their need
to receive power, Holy Ghost power to be precise; for, only He could
teach them what they really need to know to boldly live lives of victory!
Only the Holy Ghost could bring them into the saving knowledge they need to
accept deep down on the inside; unswervingly, it is the only kind of knowledge
that will set the captive, spiritually, physically, mentally and emotionally, free!

While that settled into my soul, names and faces started appearing in my mind's eye, like screen shots on an old movie reel, as the title of this poem came to me; that's when, I felt the impetus to begin to pray for them to be filled with the Holy Ghost. After that, I went on with the rest of my morning routine that occurs when getting ready for church; to that end, I fed my ten year old kitties; and, as everything else was in place, I could perform those tasks on autopilot, I began to coast.

• • • • • • • • • • •

Michelle Louise Pierre

After praise and worship, which was determinedly geared up to do battle in the
name of the LORD, Pastor Tim stepped to the podium and told us he would
be preaching on the Holy Ghost; I had to shout in agreement, "Amen!"
As he began to preach, and You moved, it was a total confirmation
of what we, You and I, had been talking about for the last week,
culminating in morning prayers being prayed for friend and kin.

The sermon was all about knowing who we are in Christ Jesus,
regardless of the opinion of man, and that, first and foremost, we need
to be baptized with the Holy Ghost, as Jesus spoke of in Acts 1: 3 – 5 & 8.
That baptism is filled with God's omnipotent power, which completely nullifies
the enemy's inroads to your mind; therefore, bringing with it wisdom directly from
the throne of grace, to move us out of confusion and stagnation, before it is too late.

The sermon ended with an altar call for all those, who had the desire to be baptized
with the Holy Ghost and power, to come forth, hands raised in supplication,
and hearts open to receive this precious gift, which is freely available to us, all.
My heart almost burst with joy, as I held back the tears, when one of those
I had prayed for this very morning, came walking straight down the aisle
to take a place in the front, eyes closed, hands raised, heeding the call.

●　　●　　●　　●　　●　　●　　●　　●

My God, my God, my God, I just have to bow in reverence to You, for the way You so sovereignly
moved through the hearts of Your children, today, while aligning us in The Spirit to the point that we
were chosen to be used, in the name of Jesus, then get out of Your way, and let Your holy will transpire.
Dear Father God, all's I can say, in agreement with Your divine will, is that You are totally awesome,
and it is a true pleasure to give You all the praise, worship and honor You are due; continue to, in
all-power, baptize Your children, who will surrender to You, with the Holy Ghost and with fire!

July 29, 2018 – Sunday
(From The Book – A Consuming Fire)

In A Solitary Way

<u>BEFORE</u>

Before I met you, I truly thought
I knew what love was all about.
I thought that I had been in love
before, and that without a doubt.

Now, I find myself looking back over my life,
knowing that I have never been in this place before.
For loving you, my Dear Husband To Be, will have opened
places that I didn't even know were behind those closed doors.

May the LORD, whom we both serve, love and adore, be our
mainstay as we walk, separately, in the Spirit, right now.
In the name of Jesus, may He continue to sustain us though the
lonely nights of our longing souls, for truly only He knows how.

Dear LORD, bless us in the waiting process with Your healing, delivering,
purging, restorative, redemptive love, that grows stronger every day.
Continue to birth in our hearts this new, pure love for each other
that grows more intense, when we read Your Word, fast and pray.

Thank You, Father God, for being with us along each turn and bend,
as we go about our daily lives, which at times seems like just another chore.
For we both know that without Your hand of mercy guiding us through,
we will never meet, and things will just continue on, as before.

July 18, 2006 – Tuesday

Michelle Louise Pierre

BLESS HIM, TODAY

Whatever is in my future husband's heart today
If it is not of You, Dear Lord, cast it away
Enfold him in Your sheltering love, where he needs to stay
In Jesus' holy name, I pray

If the path he's on will lead him to sin
Take him off it Lord, forgive him and let him start over again
This time going the way, of repentance, that You have placed within
In Jesus' holy name, I pray

If love of flesh is leading him around like a tourist in a strange, fascinating land
Show him, that true love can only be found nestled in Your omniscient hand
Love that is formed, molded, mended and healed according to Your divine plan
In Jesus' holy name, I pray

When old heart wounds rise to cause him to doubt
Show him that Your love for him, will assuredly chase all of the hurt out
Then teach him to stand in faith, knowledge, wisdom and in victory shout
In Jesus' holy name, I pray

Also, let him feel Your love and the love You are nurturing in my heart for him
Teach him to pray, fast and walk as a soul saved, by the touch of Your garment's hem
Assure him in the hope of a bright future, causing past failures to grow blessedly dim
In Jesus' holy name, I pray

And, above all, birth in him a love for all things sacred, holy and sanctified by You
Correct his vision, so that he can see what it is that he has still yet to do
Before you will let him find me, the one who will love him as You have taught her, too
In Jesus' holy name, I pray

Amen

December 20, 1997 – Saturday
(From The Book – The God Of All Comfort)

In A Solitary Way

BLESS MY HUSBAND

Philemon 6
That the communication of thy faith may become effectual by the
acknowledging of every good thing which is in you in Christ Jesus.

Hebrews 11: 1
Now faith is the substance of things hoped for,
the evidence of things not seen.

Bless my husband, oh Lord, with what You
have lain aside for him to receive this day.
Bless him from head to toe as he digs deeper
into Your Word, seeking nuggets of truth, I pray.

Because You are maturing me, I don't need
to see his face, or even know his name.
I simply ask that You cleanse his heart
and mind, right now, with Your holy flame.

If he is lonely, at this moment, assure him
that You are preparing for him, his good thing.
Let him know that she will be a cut above the rest
and will be the queen, who causes his heart to sing.

Lord, thank You, for assuring my soul that he
and I will surely, one day, meet face to face.
Thank You, for touching both of our hearts and minds,
with a divine measure of heavenly, contented grace.

Bless my husband, most of all with a fiery
passionate love for You, that never runs cold.
For when he comes to find me, let him do it as
Your royal son, not meek and mild, but bold.

March 18, 2002 – Saturday

Michelle Louise Pierre

CELIBACY'S SONG

Colossians 3: 1 & 2
If ye then be risen with Christ, seek those things which are above,
where Christ sitteth on the right hand of God. Set your
affection on things above, not on things on the earth.

Galatians 5: 24 & 25
And they that are Christ's have crucified the flesh
with the affections and lusts. If we live in
the Spirit, let us also walk in the Spirit.

Being committed to living a life consecrated to the LORD,
in every way, including the flesh, is not a stance that will
win us any popularity contests, in this world's view.
But, since that is not our true concern, Dear Single Saint, let's
pick ourselves up, seek forgiveness, repent, knock the dust off,
and get back to living the life of holiness, He has called us, too.

Still, in reality, the LORD knows, there are times when temptations
appear on the horizon, in various forms, to snag our attention away, by
focusing our affections on the things beneath, in the lonely, stark cold.
But, our Father, has cautioned us to avoid those things that can only to be
satisfied by the lust of the flesh, outside of a marriage sanctified by Him;
for, the enemy's ultimate goal is to ensnare our soul in death's numbing hold.

Let us learn to not be wise in our own fleshly conceits, to the point where we
can be so easily ensnared by a bit of flattery on the lips of someone, who most
assuredly does not know Jesus as LORD, or have our best interest at heart.
For, we are the called, according to His purpose, to show forth His glory
on this earth, and we must be strong enough to know that left to our own
devices, no good thing will prevail, when we are no longer earnestly set apart.

Adhere to the call to celibacy that weeps through our pores, even as we want
to fight it every step of the way; for, the Holy Spirit beckons, and our flesh
must again learn to be humble and yield, turning away from all that is wrong.
I pray for us all, Dear Single Saints, in the name of Jesus, that we remain firm in our
resolve to abstain from desires of the flesh that are outside of God's will, as we learn
that only in complete surrender to Him, can we, without hypocrisy, sing celibacy's song.

Hallelujah and Amen!!!

March 20, 2018 – Tuesday

In A Solitary Way

COME CORRECT, OR DON'T GET DRESSED!

I want a man, who is fully grown, spiritually
and emotionally, with his act together.
I want a man, who is free to love me, and is
fully prepared to be loved by me, forever.

I do not have time to wonder what you feel about me,
or to spend time, playing those childish dating games.
I have been set apart, called by the Lord, Most High,
to have a definite purpose and proclaim His name!

Is your calling secure in what it is,
that the Father wants you to do?
Are you actively doing what the Lord
has called you, personally, to pursue?

Or, is running after me and getting my attention,
the only meal that you want on your plate?
Have you decided, that your mission, now,
first and foremost, is to take me on a date?

Then I have some news for you, Dear Brother,
that might turn your beautiful smile upside down.
I do not want a man, who's so enamored with me, that he is
running around, doing foolish things that make him look like a clown.

And, another thing, outward appearance will only get you so far;
for, I will see what the Holy Spirit will reveal to me, about you.
Please do not spend all of your time building your worldly riches,
without letting the Holy Ghost cleanse you, through and through.

My man, has to add new dimensions to my life, as I will his,
in ways that will be creative, without being overly stressed.
My new philosophy is this, because I am tired of the mess,
"Come correct or don't bother to get dressed".

June 13, 1999 – Sunday
(From The Book – A Pen Of Iron)

Michelle Louise Pierre

CONVERSATIONS WITH GRACE

Psalm 37: 23 – 25
The steps of a good man are ordered by the LORD: and he delighteth
in his way. Though he fall, he shall not be utterly cast down: for the
LORD upholdeth him with his hand. I have been young, and now am old;
yet have I not seen the righteous forsaken, nor his seed begging bread.

Titus 2: 1 – 4
But speak thou the things which become sound doctrine: That the aged men
be sober, grave, temperate, sound in faith, in charity, in patience. The aged women
likewise, that they be in behaviour as becometh holiness, not false accusers, not given
to much wine, teachers of good things; That they may teach the young women
to be sober, to love their husbands, to love their children

Dear Most Holy High LORD, Creator of all things, who unconditionally loves us
with an everlasting love, steeped in His mercy that truly does endure forever; for,
our Father most assuredly will take nothing away from us that He will not,
in His sovereignty, meaning in whatsoever way He chooses, replace.
The Holy Spirit instructs and comforts our hearts, speaking to us as light
in the darkness, in a dying world, where the gates of hell which come against us,
but will not prevail, in our lives, no matter how firm the intent is to destroy us,
are actually dispelled by God's miraculous, omnipotent grace.

· · · · ·

I have had good fortune, over the last several months, of taking the time to talk
with two Christian women, both octogenarians, who have raised their children
to adulthood, have grandchildren of their own, and, on top of that, have
chosen to live lives as widows, for the remainder of their years.
Both of these woman, have been through their own personal trials and battles,
that come along with the passage of time; yet, they have remained strong in their
resolve to live lives that exemplify Your hand upon their hearts, in times of
unspeakable joy as well as when their eyes flooded with sorrowful tears.

My first encounter was with Auntie Rose Beasley, who, although not a blood
relative, has been considered family, for several decades, and has dispensed,
most often in a quiet, gentle way, wisdom that has been born out of a
personal relationship with the LORD, and time honored perseverance.
During that time, we were able to chat about the goodness of the LORD in
the land of the living, how He has brought us a mighty long way, as well as
how marvelous her grandsons are doing in school, along with the witty,
thought provoking things that they say, well beyond their experience.

In A Solitary Way

Encounter number two began last weekend, when I met "Mama Lou", Mrs. Louise
Campbell, living with her daughter, a new friend of mine, who moved out of town at
the end of the year; after arriving for an overnight stay, on my way to the guest
room, introductions were made, accompanied by a big hug, between she and I.
Later that evening, on what I thought was my way to bed, after midnight,
I stopped in to say, "Goodnight" and that's when the real chatting began;
before I knew it, I had taken the seat, Momma Lou had indicated next to her
on the bed, and almost five hours passed in what seemed like the blink of an eye.

•   •   •   •   •

Looking back, I feel truly blessed indeed with these divine appointments, for
that was exactly what they were, because it was the first time, I could speak about
faith so openly with older women, who also loved You, through all their mistakes and
ups and downs; for, both, settled souls, had You, sweet Jesus, in their loving hearts, abide.
At the end of both conversations infused with grace, I felt such gratitude towards You, LORD,
as residual heaviness in my soul, there since the passing of my mother, was infused with Your light,
loving touch; for, this was Your way of letting me know, You will, indeed, never leave or forsake me,
and have, in-turn, given me two wise, beautiful godly women, in whom I can now, safely confide.

Dear LORD, keep them under the shadow of Your wings, safe and secure.
I ask this in the name of Your Son, Jesus, and for His sake.
Thank You, LORD!!! Hallelujah and Amen!!!

July 27, 2018 – Friday

Michelle Louise Pierre

COUNTERFEIT LOVE

2 Corinthians 11: 12 – 15
But what I do, that I will do, that I may cut off occasion from them which desire occasion;
that wherein they glory, they may be found even as we. For such are false apostles,
deceitful workers, transforming themselves into the apostles of Christ. And no marvel;
for Satan himself is transformed into an angel of light. Therefore it is no great thing
if his ministers also be transformed as the ministers of righteousness;
whose end shall be according to their works.

The relationship was built in heaven, or so you
thought, for it looked like the real thing from the inside.
Now, look a little closer and you can see into the places where
the focus should have been narrow, it was actually wide.

He said that he loved you, yet within
months, turned and walked away.
Leaving you, alone, again to fall
on your face; now, fast and pray.

Things have gone full circle, and all that you can do
is repent, seek forgiveness and, once again, turn.
Thank You, LORD, for deliverance from a trip,
fueled by your flesh, to cause you to eternally burn.

Now, forgiven, and forgiving, the Holy Spirit can call to
remembrance what true love is, when it comes from above.
Now, stay under God's divine protection, don't stray, and you
will never, again, succumb to the lure of counterfeit love.

January 15, 2006 – Sunday

In A Solitary Way

DARE I...

Dear LORD, dare I fall in love, again, with the one
You are so graciously preparing to send into my life?
Dare I hope in a future with him, that will
last a forever lifetime, as husband and wife?

Dare I let go and let You, heavenly Father,
order his steps straight to my heart?
Dare I dream of being with him, and placing
past things behind, letting You set us apart?

Dare I trust that You will be in the midst of this
relationship, and have preordained it to be so?
Dare I abandon myself in You, allowing what
will be tenderly birthed in my heart, to freely grow?

Dare I allow You, Holy Spirit, to speak to my soul,
telling me to trust You, for this time it will be all right?
Dare I start readjusting my thinking to make room
for him in my thoughts, both day and night?

I do dare, for You, sweet Jesus, are making intercession
on our behalf, and will guide us in how we must proceed.
Dear LORD, thank You for not giving us a spirit of fear, but of
power, love and a sound mind, for on You, we will stand, indeed.

July 18, 2006 – Tuesday

Michelle Louise Pierre

DATING IN THE DARK

Matthew 7: 13 & 14
Enter ye in at the strait gate: for wide is the gate, and broad is the way, that leadeth to destruction, and many there be which go in thereat: Because straight is the gate, and narrow is the way, which leadeth unto life, and few three be that find it.

I saw him walking down the street
and he gave me a curious glance as
he smiled, before saying, "Hi".
His voice sounded so sweet,
I couldn't help but to smile back,
and give him a similar reply.

Sometime later, after I had entered
a store, I noticed him, again, but
this time, he came right up to me.
He asked me if he could talk
to me for a while, because he felt
that he would like to get to know me.

I responded that it was okay; he seemed
harmless enough and he was rather
nice looking, upon closer glance.
We talked for a while about this and that; then,
when I started to leave, he inquired, if I would
give him my phone number, by any chance.

Now, we have been "talking" for a while;
in the process, we are really getting to
know and like each other, a lot.
We have so much in common, but there is that
one little matter that is a bone of contention;
for, you see, I'm a Christian and he is not.

Well, I haven't really shared with
my girlfriends from church,
that I am even talking to this man.
Some of them are starting to get suspicious,
because when they invite me somewhere,
I have to tell them that I have other plans.

Then, I leave, real quick before they can question me
any further; for you see, he and I have, now, started
to date and I sometimes have to squeeze church in.
He keeps telling me that he wants to meet, all of my
friends, because I have already met all of his; frankly,
I am afraid to bring him around my saved friends.

In A Solitary Way

This duplicitous lifestyle is starting to take
a strange turn, and I am finding that it is also
taking a rather negative toll on my spiritual walk.
By the nature of our intense relationship, I am
finding less time for devotion, because conviction
greets me with every Word and/or verse, and I balk.

So, I've put my Bible down, for now, which
is okay, I am sure, because Jesus knows that
I love Him, with all of my heart and soul.
He understands that I have not had feelings
like this, for any man, in a very long time,
and it's okay, I can keep them under control.

Well, I have noticed that things are starting
to change for the better, and for the worse,
all seemingly at the same momentous time.
Now that I have agreed to one day marry him,
he is making many more demands upon me, and
his emotions seem to be "turning on a dime".

I finally gave in, and invited him to church, to
officially show him off, ring on finger, to all of
my sisters and brothers in the Lord , as my fiancé.
A few of them called me later, to ask me where
I had met him and was he actually saved, because they
noticed how he had acted, when the pastor began to pray.

I told them, that they simply didn't understand
how much he truly and sincerely loves me,
and that he is a very affectionate guy.
That's why, he was more interested in whispering
sweet nothings in my ear, than he was in being moved
by the sister, next to me, who had begun to cry.

Well, the wedding date is coming up and I find that
I spend a lot more time crying, than I do making
plans, like all of the other happy brides to be.
I am also finding that we are spending a lot of time
arguing over whether or not, after the marriage, he will
allow the Lord into his heart, thereby setting him free.

This whole thing is becoming more than I can handle, on my
own; so conviction or not, I decided to go back to reading
my Word, daily, while checking for an answer to this mess.
Now, I can finally, see that this has been a slippery road
that I have been on all of these past months, and it has
left me shattered, confused and anything but blessed.

Michelle Louise Pierre

Still, with all the things that I have been up to, since I met
this man, I have repented, and have found that forgiveness is
still available to me; for, all that I had to do was, sincerely, ask.
Now, the Lord is washing my soul clean, from the intimacies
of a relationship built not upon the rock of Jesus Christ,
my Risen Savior and King, while I was "off task".

Further, I honestly admit that he carried a certain charm
that appealed to the sensual side of my nature, which I
thought I had gotten beyond needing to keep in-check.
That particular angel of light, sent by the enemy, slipped
right in through my defenses, because I had felt like
I needed a little fun in my life, and hey, what the heck!

I wanted to remain friends, with him, even though
I had to call the wedding off, but he has made it very
clear, to me, what type of "friendship" he wants.
According to him, friendship carries with it a greater
price, on the intimate side, than I will ever, again, pay,
because I am not willing to go back to those past haunts.

Backslider though I was, I am finally back under the protective
covering of the Lord, and I thank Him, every moment,
for rescuing me from the foolish leanings of my own heart.
I am finding that I have a renewed zeal for the Word of God,
too, and I am so grateful that I was not lost out there,
as I stumbled around blindly yoked to a sin laden cart.

In retrospect, that relationship had been, like driving around in a crowed
parking lot at the mall, on a beautiful day, while moving along the
rows of cars, seeing no empty spaces, as if lost in the dark.
Now, I can see that I had merely sought the closest spot,
even if I did have to squeeze into it, because I thought that it
was better than continuing to wait for, a better place to park.

2 Corinthians 6: 14 – 16
*Be ye not unequally yoked together with unbelievers: for what fellowship hath
righteousness with unrighteousness? and what communion hath light with darkness?
And what concord hath Christ with Belial? or what part hath he that believeth
with an infidel? And what agreement hath the temple of God with idols?
for ye are the temple of the living God; as God hath said, I will dwell in them,
and walk in them ; and I will be their God, and they shall be my people.*

September 16, 1999 – Thursday
(From The Book – A Pen Of Iron)

In A Solitary Way

DEAR LORD, THE MAN

Dear LORD, the man, whom You are preparing for me will be much more
than I could have ever, in my wildest imagination, hoped or dreamed.
He will allow Your love to shine forth through him, as You continue
to churn us both, so that we will rise together as holy cream.

LORD, thank You for, in Your sovereign mercy, reaching down to arrest us
from going astray, leading us straight back to You, and, one day, to one another.
Thank You, for nurturing within us a love that seemingly came out of nowhere
and was instantly birthed, in our bosoms as friends, allies, sister and brother.

LORD, under Your leadership we will learn that the enemy, we must continue
to fight, is the subtle one, who would seek to divide us, to keep us apart.
LORD, continue sparking within us the impetus to fight in the Spirit, and to challenge
the enemy head on, as You stoke the battle cry of praise and worship right from the start!

We were created to praise You, oh LORD and be in everlasting fellowship
with You, in such a way that nothing could hinder, squelch, destroy or interfere.
Dear LORD, continue Your healing work in our hearts, bodies, minds and souls,
as You, alone, fine tune, under the unction of the Holy Ghost, our spiritual ears.

Help us to look out for one another, while listening intently to Your voice, so that
what we do, as a sanctified couple for Your Kingdom, will never be done in vain.
LORD, we love You intimately, as singles, and will be further humbled by the endearing
love You will give us for each other, that will truly be better than any former rain.

Help us to stay the course that You have lain out for us to follow, as we,
Your sheep, are guided by Your rod and staff, according to Your holy plan.
LORD, may we never cease to praise and worship You, as we submit to Your
authority, allowing You to cement our spirits together as, mere, woman and man.

Dear Father, this is not something that we could ever have hoped to achieve on our
own, for we know that without Your breath of life, we are nothing but dust and dirt.
LORD, continue to strengthen us in our inner man, as the love You will bless us
with, is being birthed as sweetly and tenderly as a new born babe, on this earth.

July 18, 2006 – Tuesday

Michelle Louise Pierre

DEEP CALLETH UNTO DEEP

Psalm 42: 7
Deep calleth unto deep at the noise of thy waterspouts:
all thy waves and thy billows are gone over me.

The sun is desperately trying
to peek tenderly through
a mountain of fog and smog,
to brighten up a dreary day

Autumn leaves have fallen

Spring buds are grasping tenderly
towards the sun as nature sings
imperceptibly, in anticipation
of full glorious bloom

Strip away the results of
our foolishness, Dear Jesus,
God's Only Begotten Son

Let us see the bright
glorious light of
this wonderfully
God kissed new day

Just like the omnipotent voice
of God sets the seasons aright

LORD, place within each of us, while
solitary souls, a holy call that also runs deep
and can only be answered by our own spirits

March 21, 1998 – Saturday
(From The Book – The God Of All Comfort)

In A Solitary Way

DIVINE PROTECTION

Psalm 91: 9 – 11
Because thou hast made the LORD,
which is my refuge, even the most High,
thy habitation; There shall no evil befall thee,
neither shall any plague come nigh thy dwelling.
For he shall give his angels charge over thee,
to keep thee in all thy ways.

Dear LORD, thank You for keeping my future Honey,
safe, now and forever, as You in sovereignty lead,
direct and guide him, throughout his day.
For You have most assuredly given us the very
hosts of heaven to protect us from the snares of
the fowler, as we humble our hearts to pray.

Precious Holy Ghost, may the study of the Word, along
with a constant stream of prayer, praise and worship,
always fill our hearts, both now and in the future.
May the love that You, Dear Father, have so miraculously
given us for one another, be the type that will last a lifetime,
held together by Your heavenly crafted suture.

For I know that he loves You, first and foremost, and
wants to be the best provider, husband and giver to Your
Kingdom, that You have been teaching him how to be.
On my part, You have been preparing me like You
did Esther, with the heart of a kitten, turned lioness,
to wage war, to minister to souls, which is our destiny.

For we both know that we will be put together as a
Spirit-baptized couple, not just to fulfill our need
for human love, but to let Your will be done.
We know that we are especially chosen by You, to
do an even greater work for You, than either of us
could have achieved as singles, when we become one.

LORD, continuously keep him hidden under the shadow
of Your wings, as You instruct him in the night seasons,
with coals of fire, purifying his heart, mind, body and soul.
Protect the tender grapes of these lessons learned at the foot of
Your throne, as he walks into my life, fully shod in the manner You
intended, learning how to daily relinquish to You, full control.

In the name of Jesus, I pray that You continuously keep
Your loving arms of divine protection around us, keeping away
derision that would try to shatter our love for You, and for one another.
Continuously build in us the desire to stay in Your most holy faith,
as we conduct our lives as saints of God, knowing we've been granted
this precious gift of love, mercy, grace and divine favor, like no other.

Thank You, LORD!!!
Amen and Amen!!!

October 21, 2006 – Saturday

In A Solitary Way

__ENOUGH!__

Mark 4: 2 - 8
And he taught them many things by parables, and said unto them in his doctrine,
Hearken; Behold, there went out a sower to sow: And it came to pass, as he sowed,
some fell by the way side, and the fowls of the air came and devoured it up.
And some fell on stony ground, where it had not much earth; and immediately
it sprang up, because it had no depth of earth: But when the sun was up,
it was scorched; and because it had no root, it withered away. And some fell
among thorns, and the thorns grew up, and choked it, and it yielded no fruit.
And other fell on good ground, and did yield fruit that sprang up and increased;
and brought forth, some thirty, and some sixty, and some an hundred.

In the midst of re-editing this book, my mother passed from this life
into eternity, three weeks ago, today; and, now that I can focus,
again, I wanted to take the time to capture what I have been
feeling during this time, as it flows through my heart.
However, before I tap into those emotions, I must backtrack
to over five years ago, when I had a life changing decision
to make, as to whether I would retire after over thirty years
of working, and from that season in my life, depart.

I remember one day walking around my home, with my
two cats as silent witnesses, as I came down my hallway,
while praying to the LORD, about whether I would be able
to afford to actually do it, or would it actually be too tough.
As I stressed and pondered over the ins and outs of my finances,
as a single woman, I found myself pausing in midstride, and
that is when I heard God speak to me and say one simple,
yet extremely profound, word, "Enough".

Right then and there, a calmness came over my soul
and I knew that all my worries, and worldly machinations,
had all been in vain, for He would do what He has always done,
which has been to, in divine excellence, take care of me.
Now, almost five years after retiring, without ever working
any "side jobs", I find myself in a place of contentment and
overall well-being, that I have never been in before, for I am
not bound up in the stifling grief of regret, but free.

Now, to the present moment, I have shared this with very few of people,
saved and unsaved, for I have found that people tend to speak to you, with
their actions or inability to act, out of their fear, not out of their faith, in times
like these that can engender, in most, such crippling heartache and strife.
I find them looking at me as though I should be curled into a fetal position
that they need to pray me out of; even after I share with them that my mom
is in heaven, while grief pours off them in cloying waves and they reach out
to "suffocatingly" clutch me in their arms, speaking words of death, not life.

At those times, I plead the blood of Jesus over me; for, to me, this is where "the rubber meets the road" in this Christian faith walk for believers, who claim to love the LORD in a way that supersedes all but the desire to see Jesus, one day, face to face, regardless of worldly stuff.
I desire to be a hundred-fold witness of Your immutable grace on this earth, as the Holy Spirit, the Comforter, truly has comforted my heart, encapsulating me in a cushion of peace, love and joy that has proven, in all situations, even in the harsh reality of death, the LORD is truly enough!

April 23, 2018 – Monday

In A Solitary Way

FATHER, IS HE THE ONE?

Luke 7: 20 - 22
When the men were come unto him, they said, John Baptist hath sent us
unto thee, saying, Art thou he that should come? or look we for another?
And in that same hour he cured many of their infirmities and plagues,
and of evil spirits; and unto many that were blind he gave sight.
Then Jesus answering said unto them, Go your way, and tell John what
things ye have seen and heard; how that the blind see, the lame walk, the lepers
are cleansed, the deaf hear, the dead are raised, to the poor the gospel is preached.

Dear Father God, is he the one, for whom
I have been praying all of these many years?
Is his the face, that I could never have imagined,
seeing, through eyes once awash with tears?

Is he the one, who will be the representation
of Your love, manifested in flesh and bone?
Are his arms the ones that will encircle me,
letting me know that I will never again, be alone?

Is he the one, whose love will satisfy me completely
and totally, leaving room for no other, even in thought?
Has his life been purchased by the blood of Jesus;
has this man, truly been by Your Son's blood, bought?

LORD, I am trusting You to be squarely in the
midst of this relationship, that has just begun.
For You have reminded me, this night, if the
fruit of his life checks out, then he is the one.

September 27, 2006 – Wednesday

Michelle Louise Pierre

FOR, THIS IS THE WILL OF GOD

Hebrews 11: 1 – 3
Now faith is the substance of things hoped for, the evidence of things not seen.
For by it the elders obtained a good report. Through faith we understand
that the worlds were framed by the word of God, so that things which
are seen were not made of things which do appear.

Child, in singleness, I need you to walk circumspectly
in the sight of all men, allowing Me to shine through.
Hold your head up, shoulders back, for, this is the will
of God in Christ Jesus, My little one, concerning you.

I need you to stand firmly on My Word, nothing wavering, holding
fast to the promises, I have made you in the seasons of the night.
Do not look at the situation with the eyes of the flesh, for
when reasoning with the carnal mind, it will never look right.

You must claim the victory now, over this situation,
and call it done in the name of Jesus Christ, the LORD.
Plead His blood against this enemy, for only that given
in sacrificial love, can break this stronghold's binding cord.

Know that it is the ultimate, faultless will of God, the Father,
that you will have victory over every trick of the enemy.
Now, get back in His Word and into intimate fellowship with Him,
for being defeated, unlike God's foes, is not your divine destiny.

October 25, 2006 – Wednesday

FREEING YOU, TO LOVE

Heart beating,
strongly in
my chest.
My God, I give
You my all, I give
You my best.

Set my desire
on You, set my
soul aflame.
Whatever it takes,
do it Lord, I desire
to change my name.

Name me, according
to the grace and purpose,
You have for my life.
Wed me to You,
oh Lord, before I
become this man's wife.

He is waiting to approach me
and reveal himself to me,
as directed by Your voice.
He has set his affections upon
me, because of You, I have
become his ultimate choice.

I can see him coming, filled
with Your precious Spirit,
to find me, his good thing.
My heart already belongs to
You, You are the only one,
who causes my soul to sing.

Dear Lord, how do I make
room for him in my heart,
and not leave You out?
How do I cleave to him and not
lose my hold on You; thereby,
opening the door to doubt?

Michelle Louise Pierre

Daughter, I am expanding
your heart as I heal all of your
wounds and tattered emotions.
I have increased your capacity
to contain love; loving him, will
not rob Me of your devotions.

Loving each other, will enhance
your lives, in ways before
unknown, by either you or he.
I will continue to mature
you, together, as you both
continue to grow in Me.

Don't pull away from him,
daughter, he is the one, whom
I have graciously sent.
Accept him, in My love,
get ready to build your lives
together, expand your tent.

Take his hand, daughter, now,
in My Presence, you will both
need to permanently stay.
Let go of your mistakes,
My son and My daughter,

I am freeing you
to love, this day.

December 2, 1998 – Wednesday
(From The Book – Heart Songs Of A Poet)

In A Solitary Way

GET BACK UP!

Psalm 116: 5
Gracious is the LORD, and righteous; yea, our God is merciful.
The LORD preserveth the simple: I was brought low, and he helped me.

Saved, sanctified, filled with the Holy Ghost
Feeling lonely, depressed
Lost in a crowd of happy souls
Isolated by thoughts that only you can hear
Praying seemingly to a wall of brass
Made all the more impenetrable
By desires outside of God's will
Not knowing how to make your way back
How to reposition yourself in front of God's throne
Surely, He does not love you anymore
How could He, after what you have done?

Time spent, wasted, chasing shadows in the wind
Being pursued by figures out of your own darkness
Bleakness, despair, shame, guilt surround your heart
You have made a colossal mistake
You invested your trust in the wrong bank account
An account built upon mere flesh and bone
An account that promised yields, before unknown
Yields higher, than your own inflated expectations
Could have ever possibly dreamed up

A neon sign of false gain, temporarily blinded your sight
The Holy Spirit ignored so many times
He can no longer, by you, be heard
The still small voice
Muted out by the glitter of potential reward

All that has now drastically changed
Now, truth has willed-out and come to light
Investment lost, demolished, destroyed
Plans shattered like a beautiful vase falling on a hardwood floor
Dreams dissipated like clouds in the wind
The sun has come and consumed them, burned them away

Seen in the true light of day, you feel foolish
Self-recrimination, the likes of which can only be obtained from hindsight
Beats savagely upon your weary soul, trying to claim you as another victim
Clawing maniacally at you, as if trying to rip you to shreds
Tattered and torn, your soul bleeds
End of your rope, finally reached
Nowhere to go but up

Michelle Louise Pierre

Pride wounded, but not fatally so
You lift up your head
Digging deeply within the forsaken chambers of your mind
You decide your priorities need to change
God used to be first
Somehow His position was usurped

You still your soul, quieting your mind
Face down on the carpet
Hot tears fueled by accusations hurled directly at the Lord
Your soul pours out its bitter complaints
Like sewage seeping out of a drain

Once all of the garbage is out, nothing left to say
Exhausted, weary from the catharsis
Mind finally spinning down to a full stop
God can now begin to speak

He does not even respond to your former accusations
They are not His main concern
You have behaved like a petulant child, who has broken a forbidden toy
One that your parents had previously told you not to touch
He, instead, issues a stern rebuke that gets right to the heart of the matter
Breaking through the coldness, hardness of your greedy, unrepentant heart
He touches your heart and fills it with His love
A penetrating warmth begins to radiate within
A new river of tears flow from your already puffy eyes
He reminds you that He has been there all along
Through all of your convoluted twists and turns
Waiting, patiently by, for you to turn back to Him

Repentance now has room to move
Godly sorrow wails from the inner recesses of your spirit
Gripping you as sobs permeate your inner being
You curl up tightly into the fetal position
As if seeking the comfort of the womb
Instead, truly seeking nourishment at the hands of a loving Father
He nurses you back to health, giving you back your strength
You receive His forgiveness
Finally, you rise from the floor

. . . .

This has been a long descent into a world that should no longer
Be able to permanently claim you as its own
You now realize, that you are truly His child
That He really does love you, with an everlasting love
A love that can burn away the dross in your life

In A Solitary Way

He has enabled you to triumph over your self-inflicted pain
Even over your impetuous desires to take charge of your own life
To bring about success gauged upon worldly standards of acceptability, status

Fortified by intense love, hope and gratitude
Allowing Him to position your feet back on the right path
You receive His forgiveness, running into His outstretched arms
The Holy Spirit's voice can now direct each step, again

This lesson has been learned and stored away
Achieved through the arena of repentance
In true humility, opening yourself up to God's chastisement
Coupled with His unconditional healing love and forgiveness
Knowing that no matter what, as long as there is breath in your body
God's magnificent, unfailing love will always be there
For, surely there is no repentance received, or accepted, from the grave

You now realize that, it is not the slipping and falling
That brings about feelings of separation from God
It is simply the failure to acknowledge the fact
That when you do take that plunge
You need to seek the Lord's divine, sovereign forgiveness
Through the avenues of sincere humility and repentance

Once obtained
Secure it in your heart
Learn the lesson
Dry your eyes

Then child
Get back up!

October 28, 1996 – Monday
(From The Book – The God Of All Comfort)

Michelle Louise Pierre

GOD SAID, "NO", AGAIN!

Revelation 3: 19 – 21
As many as I love, I rebuke and chasten: be zealous therefore, and repent.
Behold, I stand at the door, and knock: if any man hear my voice, and open
the door, I will come in to him, and will sup with him, and he with me.
To him that overcometh will I grant to sit with me in my throne, even as
I also overcame, and am set down with my Father in his throne.

Wedding invitations in trembling hands, for
something is out of order and does not feel right.
The soul wrenching decision is pending as to whether
to call a halt to this impending wedding, this night.

Meeting as a couple, with the pastor, at first
seems to be just what you desperately need.
Yet, on the way to the truck, it all begins to unravel, again,
while on Jesus and His blood, you begin to drive and plead.

The ride back to your separate homes is filled with extreme tension,
with you gripping the steering wheel and earnestly praying all the way.
Knowing, instinctively in your heart, that with his own words,
and actions, the wedding must be called off, today!

That was not an easy decision to make, but one
that brought with it a release in my spirit.
LORD, thank You, for lovingly drawing me back
into fellowship with You, where I could actually get it.

Thank You, LORD, for bringing me back into focus, so that
I could repent and see where I went off track, why and when.
Father God, thank You, for stepping in right on time, and strongly
impressing upon my heart that You were indeed saying, "No", again!

March 6, 2006 – Monday

In A Solitary Way

HAPPY VALENTINE'S DAY

"Happy Valentine's Day",
all around you, say.
Whose your valentine,
single heart in dismay?
There is no one special
in your life, today.

Another day for inner desires,
dreams to crash and burn.
Where is your valentine
sweetheart, for which you yearn?
Shouldn't you just give up hope,
will you ever learn?

God is still on the throne and
He does know your need?
He has heard you in the still
of the night, earnestly plead.
He is not slack in His promises,
by word, action or deed.

Still, you wait and pray for the
day when your mate will appear.
Allow the Lord to love you
as He holds your fate so dear.
When confusion and loneliness
come, draw even more near.

Dear Lord, Jesus, teach us how
to wait in a state of grace.
Protect our tender hearts, so
discouragement can have no place.
Comfort us, now, teach us how
to love Your holy, sweet embrace.

In Your Son, Jesus' holy
and matchless name, I pray.
Amen.

February 13, 2002 – Wednesday

Michelle Louise Pierre

HEART OF MY HEART

Heart of my heart
and soul of my soul.
Sweet mysteries, together,
with God's lead, we will unfold.

Layer by layer, our love
will be wondrously exposed.
Our lives will be open to each other,
nothing hidden, nothing enclosed.

Your eyes will see my love,
and be enveloped in my allure.
I will be enraptured by your manliness,
needing no other, for sure.

God will be our guide as the miracles
savored in waiting, He outpours.
There will be no need for fighting over
what is mine and what is yours.

Our love, ordained by the Holy Father,
is from heaven, high up above.
Single now, unable to fully comprehend what
manner, this love between us, will really be of.

I know that it will be glorious and wonderful;
for, you see, the Lord has told me so.
In the wee hours of the night, He has not ceased
to encourage my heart, as I, in Him, continue to grow.

He has told me that you also are being very well prepared
by Him, to take your place and be ready to do your part.
I will continue to pray for you, daily, as the Lord leads,
for one day you will truly be heart of my heart.

March 11, 2000 – Saturday
(From The Book – Heart Song Of A Poet)

HELLO, SELF!

James 1: 21 – 25
Wherefore lay apart all filthiness and superfluity of naughtiness,
and receive with meekness the engrafted word, which is able to
save your souls. But be ye doers of the word, and not hearers only,
deceiving your own selves. For if any be a hearer of the word,
and not a doer, he is like unto a man beholding his natural
face in a glass: For he beholdeth himself, and goeth his way,
and straightway forgetteth what manner of man he was. But
whoso looketh into the perfect law of liberty, and continueth
therein, he being not a forgetful hearer, but a doer
of the work, this man shall be blessed in his deed.

Love reunited, after so much time apart
Blessed in heart, body and soul
Learning to tenderly reach out in love to You
To fall in love with You and Your special touch
Lord, You have finally become my, all and all

Sweet words of praise and adoration fill my mind
Love songs laid dormant for so many years
Words placed in my soul by You
Placed there before I was even a thought
Before, in fact, time could even begin

Tears spilling down my cheeks
Heart blessed to the max
Body warmed from the fire within
The fire of Your Holy Presence
Speaking lovingly to my mended heart

Created to praise You
Now capable of fulfilling that role
Worshipping with wisdom, understanding
Not just for things done
For the You, whom You are to me

Restored back to the wholeness of my origin
The whole person, whom I was predestined to be
To be called holy, perfected at Your hand
Jesus' sacrificial loving blood, cleansing me along the way
Hallelujahs flood my soul, causing my feet to dance

In loving gratitude to the Father, causing me to be twice born
Forgiving me, giving me another chance at happiness, joy
Learning to do things, this time, led on by the Holy Ghost
Healing me deeply within the innermost chambers of my soul
Restoring not only the joy, reacquainting me with myself

• • • • •

The self, who You
created me to be

The self, who longed so
many years to be free

The self, who desired even
in darkness to know Thee

The self, who almost gave up on life,
but You did not give up on me

The self, who had no idea how sweet
a godly life, with You, would truly be

March 15, 1999 – Monday
(From The Book – While I Have My Being)

In A Solitary Way

I AM A WALL

Song Of Solomon 8: 10
I am a wall, and my breasts like towers:
then was I in his eyes as one that found favour.

The Lord is keeping me under the shadow of His wings,
for I have allowed Him to place a wall around me.
I am not moved by every man, who is attractive,
or attracted, because I honor none above Thee.

Perfect, no way, for I have fallen a time or two, on this
holiness highway, while following my own heart's pulses.
Yet, He has forgiven me and given me the wisdom to now
know where to draw the line, on my fleshly impulses.

Only the Lord could have given me the self-control I needed
to not lie down with another man, outside of marriage.
He has gifted me with a joy overflowing and the
contented peace that can be visibly seen in my carriage.

Hallelujah, oh Lord, for using this time of singleness to
bring to full birth in my heart, a love for You and for myself.
Thank You, for encouraging me to not succumb to soulish
urges, that are best left for now, on a back shelf.

Thank You, Lord, for now I will be able to present my body to my
husband on our wedding night, without guilt or shame, at all.
Thank You, Lord, for keeping me in Your tender care, until I could
fully comprehend the inherent blessings received from being a wall.

August 5, 2002 – Monday
(From the Book – Heart Songs Of A Poet)

Michelle Louise Pierre

I AM LOOKING FOR JESUS!

I am looking for Jesus, therefore, I am not concerned with what kind of
manmade packaging you will come wrapped in, because you see He must
be abiding inside of you, lovingly shining back at me, from your eyes.
I do not want to get caught up in semantics and rationalizations, again;
for, I should not have to try to figure out if you truly are a child
of the living God, or merely a wolf in sheep's disguise.

I am looking for Jesus in the way that you walk, the manner in
which you talk, in public and behind closed doors, as well as the
things that stir, and awaken, in the imaginations of your heart.
I want to see, if you say one thing, meaning quite another, because you
are double minded, being completely unstable in all of your ways,
and have learned to turn double talk, into a way of art.

I am looking for Jesus in you, because He is telling me the work that the Holy Ghost
is doing in my heart, makes Him shine forth in me; therefore, I am to, never again,
be unequally yoked, which only serves to pull me completely off-course.
My prayer and hope is that you, too, my future husband, have been given
the same revelation and will know me, as well, because you will see our
LORD flowing through me naturally, without pretense or force.

So, until we meet, My Darling Heart, and begin to plan our life together, to become
a couple, who will love each other above all, as we storm the gates of hell to set the
captives free, in the matchless name of Jesus, our risen LORD, Savior and King;
Let us be about our Father's business so that He will be well pleased with us,
individually, while we await the blessing of one day, with our eye's focused
on Him, and each other, hear the wedding march, this time, for us, ring.

January 24, 2006 – Tuesday

In A Solitary Way

I CAN FEEL YOUR HEART

1 Samuel 16: 7
But the LORD said unto Samuel, Look not on his countenance,
or on the height of his stature; because I have refused him:
for the LORD seeth not as man seeth; for man looketh on
the outward appearance, but the LORD looketh on the heart.

Woke up this morning offering praise,
worship and sweet adoration to the LORD.
Honey, He will knit our hearts solidly together,
bringing us in line with His holy, preordained accord.

Two definitely have a better reward for their labor, and
in His sovereignty, He will bind us with His threefold cord.
He will restore youthful desires, tailoring them in such a
way that with each other's love, we will never be bored.

LORD, this will truly be a miracle that You will have bestowed
upon us, as You, alone, set this divine future appointment.
Blessed be Your holy name, heavenly Father, for the
precious gift of Your Son, Jesus, given to us with godly intent.

Thank You, Holy Ghost, for building within us a love, birthed
in the flames, that will stand the test of time, as You meant.
LORD, help us to stay on this predestined course that will lead to true
humility and submission, as when needed, we wholeheartedly repent.

LORD, thank You for every storm that You have brought us through,
in our single lives, giving us, each time a chance at a fresh new start.
Thank You, for guiding us, by example, in the way that we should
love each other, unconditionally, for it will truly be a God-given art.

Continue to soften the rough edges in our lives, born out of the need
to survive, submitting instead to You, becoming sanctified and set apart.
Dear LORD, thank You for the love of this man, I will honor and respect, for
I will feel passion, compassion and tenderness, coming straight from his heart.

October 21, 2006 – Saturday

Michelle Louise Pierre

I FELL IN LOVE, TODAY, AGAIN

Softly and tenderly, He looked my way.
Swooning slightly, body began to sway.

Tongue heavy as lead, what could I say?
Eyes captivated, soul needs to pray.

Bless the Lord, hallelujahs form on my lips.
Can't stand still, movement in my hips.

Living water in the fountain, I take a big sip.
Heart pounding, not quite ready for the trip.

Stumbling, reaching, grasping for the Savior's hem.
Voices of the world, growing strangely dim.

Love looking down at me, like a precious gem.
Wanting only, more and more, of the radiance of Him.

Today is the day I have said another, "Yes" to You.
Choosing to make a payment on what is due.

Ledger never balanced, all the way through.
Knowing I need to stick with You, like glue.

Repentant, receiving forgiveness, for my present sin.
Arising, walking in faith, I have let Jesus back in.

Restored to wholeness, cleansed deeply within.
Unashamedly His, falling in love, today, again.

Song of Solomon 7:10
I am my beloved's, and his desire is toward me.

September 7, 2001 – Friday

In A Solitary Way

I HAVE LEARNED SOME THINGS

1 Corinthians 13: 8 – 11
Charity never faileth: but whether there be prophecies, they shall fail;
whether there be tongues, they shall cease; whether there be knowledge,
it shall vanish away. For we know in part, and we prophesy in part.
But when that which is perfect is come, then that which is in part shall be
done away. When I was a child, I spake as a child, I understood as a child,
I thought as a child: but when I became a man, I put away childish things.

I have learned some things throughout all
of these, sometimes calamitous, years.

I have learned that joy does come,
in the morning, even in the midst of tears.

I have learned that waiting, builds patience and
strength, even in the face of my doubts and fears.

I have learned that heartbreak and heartache, meant to disable,
simply come to move your soul into the next set of gears.

I have learned that trouble does not last, thank You, LORD,
and the remedy is certainly not spirits, wine, or a few more beers.

I have learned that carnal love can take on many forms, but only
the love sanctified by God, will matter, for His time nears.

I have learned that drawing near to Jesus the Christ is more important
than the distraction of transient love or fickle approval from peers.

I have learned that being single is a time of true blessing that
brings focus and clarity, even amidst the lure of the wild frontiers.

I have learned that all treasure, no matter how attractive, on this earth,
is but temporary, and will one day, be like a vapor that disappears.

I have learned that the enticement of false love, is actually lust
masquerading in such a way to put my "faith bank account" in arrears.

I have learned that only what I do for Jesus will last, despite
having to face worldly contempt, condescension and jeers.

I have learned that if my eye truly be single, my whole body
will be full of the Light, that for all the world, appears.

I have learned that with Jesus as my LORD and Savior, nothing
can hinder me from obtaining Glory, unless I plug-up my ears.

I have learned that loving the LORD grows day by day, building
an intimacy that stimulates deeper depths, as my very soul cheers.

I have learned that darkness has no hold on me, unless I deliberately,
willfully, choose the wide way, that in destruction's path veers.

I have learned that my heavenly Father loves me with an everlasting love,
that transcends the valley of the shadow of death, whenever it appears.

I have learned that God's holy anointing truly does break the yoke,
while setting the captives free, as He, alone, controls and steers.

I have learned that you, too, can have the blessing of eternal life with Jesus,
if you would but surrender your hearts and humble your souls, my dears.

I have learned that death, hell, nor the grave, can hold you, because
the shed blood of Jesus bought your liberty and still, your sin, clears.

• • • • • • • •

I have truly learned some things, while walking with the LORD,
and I challenge all, to shutout the worldly chatter, so that His still,
small voice you, too, this day, will finally be able to hear.
In closing, I have also learned that praying to touch the heart of God
is not impossible to achieve, if you will but submit to His authority,
while choosing to forget those things that doggedly interfere.

July 11, 2018 – Wednesday

I MISS YOU, ALREADY

I miss you already,
but that is okay.
The ache will surely lessen,
with each passing day.

It is not like this is a place,
where I have never been before.
It's just that I hoped you were the
man, whom I could love, forevermore.

I wanted to run full throttle ahead,
loving you all the more.
But, the Lord stepped in, with revelations,
that closed my heart's once open door.

I miss you and have cried, and
will cry, for what could have been.
Wanting, hoping, then resigning
in my heart, to just be your friend.

So, even though I miss you, already, I know
that the Lord still has, for me, His ultimate best.
You and I touched hearts, ever so briefly,
but in the end that love couldn't survive the test.

Thank You, Lord, for opening my heart, to love
this man You brought in, and then out of my life.
Now, I am moving ever forward, awaiting Your presentation,
of the one, who will unequivocally, one day, call me, wife.

May 2, 2004 – Sunday

Michelle Louise Pierre

I PRESS

Philippians 3:14
I press toward the mark for the prize of the
high calling of God in Christ Jesus.

Single
I press

Lonely
I press

Discouraged
I press

Biological-clock
I press

Childless
I press

Brokenhearted
I press

Confused
I press

• • •

I am
Christ's
I press

I am
Anointed
I press

I am
Humbled
I press

I am
Saved
I press

In A Solitary Way

I am
Sanctified
I press

I am
Spirit-filled
I press

I am
Determined
I press

September 12, 1999 – Sunday
(From The Book – While I Have My Being)

Michelle Louise Pierre

I PROMISED HIM

I promised Him that when He blessed me with you, I would
love you, forever and a day, and that would never change.
I promised Him to be your wife in happy times and
even in times of bitter, cold storm and rain.

I promised Him to never to allow anger to rule my heart, or to
reject you for any reason; and, that will always remain true.
I promised Him to hold you in my arms, enveloping you tangibly
in my love, as it coursed straight through my body to you.

I promised Him to be faithful to you, and to place no one
else before you, in my affections, besides Him, our LORD.
I promised Him to stick by you, showing full support,
while allowing the Holy Ghost to keep us on one accord.

I promised Him that I would fully accept you,
as His choice for my husband, in mind, body and spirit.
I promised Him to cleave only to you, and when the
enemy raised his voice against you, I would not hear it.

I promised Him that when we became one in the flesh,
my love and passion for you, would never wane, nor cease.
I promised Him, my future husband, that my love for you
would grow day by day, and monumentally increase.

I promised Him, that I would be by your side
in sickness and in health, whether rich or poor.
I promised Him to allow no one to interfere with our
marriage; for, in their face, I would simply close the door.

I promised our heavenly Father, that I would love you, unconditionally
and with His help and guidance, daily, I know He will show me how.
I promised God, in the name of Jesus, that we would serve Him, faithfully,
until these earthly vessels have passed away, from the here and now.

I promised Him, in Jesus' holy name, and for His sake.
Amen and Amen!!!

October 21, 2006 – Saturday

I SEE YOU & I SEE YOU, TOO!

Genesis 24: 62 – 67
And Isaac came from the way of the well Lahairoi; for he dwelt in the south country.
And Isaac went out to meditate in the field at the eventide: and he lifted up his eyes,
and saw, and, behold, the camels were coming. And Rebekah lifted up her eyes,
and when she saw Isaac, she lighted off the camel. For she had said unto the servant,
What man is this that walketh in the field to meet us? And the servant had said,
It is my master: therefore she took a vail, and covered herself. And the servant told
Isaac all things that he had done. And Isaac brought her into his mother Sarah's tent,
and took Rebekah, and she became his wife; and he loved her:
and Isaac was comforted after his mother's death .

I see you there looking
like a queen, so fine.
Wondering, in my heart of hearts,
will you truly be mine?

I see you coming to pick me up for church
and, as usual, you sure do look fine.
I have been wondering to myself, after all
these months, will you ever really be mine?

Transformed, I see your hair turn from black to
gray, also a few more pounds, here and there.
Getting closer, the thrill in my heart, almost
overwhelms me, causing me to stare.

I imagine what you will look like when your hair is gray,
and you have a little extra in the middle, right there.
As you get closer to me, my heart as usual skips
a beat, and try as I might, I can't help but stare.

I thank Jesus for you, this precious jewel,
whom He has dropped so sweetly in my lap.
Lord, thank You, for awakening in me,
something that had taken a long nap.

Lord Jesus, I thank You for this man, who pursued me,
settling comfortably into my life, like a cat on a warm lap.
The Lord awakened in me, feelings for you that I have never
felt before; in fact, I thought they had taken a permanent nap.

You are now looking directly at me, and I see
the light in your eyes, brighten at my approach.
My heart is beating, out of control, as I try to
keep knees steady, prompted by my inner coach.

You are closer now and I can see that determined look on your face,
the one you get when praying, as you continue your approach.
I am wondering what you are up to, as peace settles into my soul,
prompted by the soothing, still small voice of my inner coach.

The Holy Ghost gently whispers, "It will be all right."
as I continue to advance towards you, falling to one knee.
You look startled, but pleased, as I take your
hand in mine and whisper, "Will you marry me?"

With a look of amazement, words fail, as inwardly the Lord says,
"You can trust him, it will be all right.", while you wait on one knee.
I take a deep breath, look down into your beautiful, dark eyes,
and say a tearful "Yes", to your question, "Will you marry me?".

April 16, 2003 – Wednesday

I WILL FALL INTO YOUR HEART

Psalm 37: 4 – 6
Trust in the LORD, and do good; so shalt thou dwell in the land, and verily thou shalt be fed. Delight thyself also in the LORD; and he shall give thee the desires of thine heart. Commit thy way unto the LORD; trust also in him; and he shall bring it to pass.

My Darling, when our day finally
comes, I will fall into your heart,
and there, forever, contently stay.
For then I will know, without a doubt,
you are truly the man, for whom
I did humbly and honestly pray.

I want to be with you, now,
but the LORD most certainly
has, for us, other plans.
He is, after all, in charge of this
love, as no other, and we have to
continually leave it in His hands.

I think about you and wonder what you
will be like, along with what the LORD is
working out in your life, as time gone by.
I am anticipating being in love with you,
as I sit here at my computer, unable to
do anything else but smile and sigh.

I will fall into your heart, just as
sweetly, my dear, as the LORD has
preordained, you will, into mine.
For, the God, we intimately know and serve,
certainly knows what He is doing, and the
end result will be gloriously divine.

July 18, 2006 – Tuesday

Michelle Louise Pierre

I WILL NEED YOU

I will need you in ways that I will not have imagined,
before you actually come into my life, to stay.
I will need you to step with me into our blessed future,
with the precious Holy Spirit, leading the way.

I will need you so that I may lay my head down
on your strong shoulder, and feel utterly secure.
I will need you to speak healing words of love
to my heart, that are passionate, yet pure.

I will need you as a woman needs her man,
and there is no other, who could ever suffice.
I will need you to be my king and I, your queen,
being offered to the Lord as a living sacrifice.

I will need you to take me in your arms,
to soothe away the tensions of the day.
I will need you to seek comfort in my arms,
when the world has your mind in disarray.

I will need you, Dear Heart, to trust that my
love for you, will never come to an end.
I will need you to know that wherever life takes us,
we will be together for every curve and bend.

I will need you to be strong in the Lord, and step up
to the plate, as the spiritual head of our family.
I will need you to do this, birthed out of your own
intimate relationship with our Savior, bathed in humility.

I will need you to be a man of your word
and, more importantly, His Word.
I will need you to seek first the Kingdom of God,
as He leads you by His voice, the voice, you have heard.

Most of all, I will need you to be a man of faith, fully
submitted to our Father's will, making no provision for defeat.
For, I will be the woman of God, standing at your side,
heart to heart, hand in hand, loving you, as your helpmeet.

July 18, 2006 – Tuesday

In A Solitary Way

IF WE HAD NOT BELIEVED!

Psalm 27: 13
I had fainted, unless I had believed to see the
goodness of the LORD in the land of the living.

Longing for things that seemed impossible in the
wake of things going on, seen with the natural eye
Feeling the fear, of pervasive loneliness, attempting to
creep into my heart, settling in with a mournful sigh

Almost succumbing, but hearing the voice of the LORD
speak to my heart, telling me to hold on and not faint
Then, as if out of the blue, here you come knocking on the
door of my heart, a true brother in the LORD, a fellow saint

For, all of Your children, Dear Father, who will claim Your Son,
Jesus, as Savior and LORD, are saints of the most high God
We have to desire to live our lives out, holy before You,
by submitting to Your ever gentle, heavenly prod

Still, the choice to humble ourselves under Your mighty hand,
has to be developed, by us, over the course of many years
More than likely, we have faltered, and almost completely fallen,
along the way, shedding a great many sorrowful, repentant tears

But, LORD, Your unfailing love for us has been the sustaining
power, behind all that we have done, and have yet to do
For we, both, would surely have fainted long ago, if we
had not believed, that You would surely see us through

July 18, 2006 – Tuesday

Michelle Louise Pierre

IN A SINGLE MOMENT

Psalm 46: 1 – 5
God is our refuge and strength, a very present help in trouble. Therefore will not we fear, though the earth be removed, and though the mountains be carried into the midst of the sea; Though the waters thereof roar and be troubled, though the mountains shake with the swelling thereof. Selah. There is a river, the streams whereof shall make glad the city of God, the holy place of the tabernacles of the most High. God is in the midst of her; she shall not be moved: God shall help her, and that right early.

In a single moment, a mole hill
really does seem like a mountain.
You, honestly, can't seem to focus
on drinking from the living fountain.

In a single moment, things done solo,
seem to be more than you can bear.
You, feel beat down and discouraged,
as though there is no one else to really care.

In a single moment, the Lord's still small voice is
drowned out by the sound of one heart beating, alone.
You, find it almost impossible to unload your
burdens and meet Jesus at heaven's throne.

In a single moment, the silence becomes deafening,
and praise cannot even formulate on your lips.
You, can see no good in your solitary life of celibacy,
as the enemy tries to get you to take a side trip.

In a single moment, flashbacks of times best left
buried, come to tempt your heart to stray.
You, give in for a time to those thoughts, but because
you are His, light comes in to scatter them away.

Bless the Lord, because even in the midst of
all that "noise" going on inside of your head;
You know, for a fact, that without Christ in your life,
you would surely be insane, locked-up or dead.

As that thought settles in your heart, "Amen" and
"Hallelujah" can rise, again, as was His intent.
For, with His loving help, you have now successfully
maneuvered to the glory side of this brief, single moment.

February 5, 2002 – Tuesday

IN LOVE, ALONE?

Sitting here, a little down, thinking, feeling a subtle
kind of cold, that runs deeper than skin and bone.
Missing this man terribly, as doubts try to plague
my mind, with the question, "Am I in love, alone?"

He is not a very attentive man, right now, for he seems
much too busy with other things, to check in with me.
Am I fooling myself, Lord, that this will change after marriage,
or is this just a precursor to how a life with him, will really be?

Lord, help me to see, and feel in my innermost being, that I
am not just playing games of romance with my heart, right now.
Lord, help me to praise through this, thinking on Your goodness,
as on the way to my breakthrough, in humble submission, I bow.

Touch his heart, this instant, oh Lord, with a holy release that will
take him beyond the routine of the way he is used to doing things.
Let him, feel, that this new love You have granted to us, is not
just an ordinary one, for it was predestined by the King of kings.

Let him come to the understanding that love, just like our soul and body,
needs to be nurtured and nourished, moment by moment, day by day.
Dear Heavenly Father, I submit this moment in time to You, sending
You my love, and thanking You for Yours, in Jesus' holy name, I pray.

Amen and Amen!

December 3, 2003 – Wednesday

Michelle Louise Pierre

IN THE LIGHT OF DAY

In the light of day, my heart opens to
you, and I want to melt into your arms.
In the light of day, I know that you truly
care for me, and mean me no harm.

In the light of day, the Lord can clearly
speak to me, without all of the inner chatter.
In the light of day, He speaks to me of things
that for my soul's survival, really do matter.

In the light of day, He tells me that I
must trust Him, for He has led me to you.
In the light of day, I, trembling, place my fears at
His feet, knowing in Him, I can make it through.

In the light of day, I feel your tender compassion
and know that I can trust you with my heart.
In the light of day, I thank the Lord for His forgiveness,
and yours, because it has given us a fresh new start.

Dear Lord, in Jesus' name, help me to stay in the
light of day, and remain open to following Your lead.
For in the light of day, both my heart and my head
say that with him, it is more than safe to proceed.

**Thank You, Lord, for keeping me
in the light of this new day!**

August 27, 2002 - Tuesday

In A Solitary Way

INTEGRITY

She is your sister
He is your brother
Both, born into the family of Christ
Covered with the same royal blood
Respecting them, is second nature to you
Loving the Jesus in them
Pouring out love from the Jesus in you
Not deliberately hurting them in anyway
Always able to look them directly in the eyes
Allowing them to see inside your soul
If they truly desire to get that close
Honestly seeking God's face for direction
Desiring to be encased within His loving arms

Giving your word, backing it up with action
Not shirking your duties, seeking ways of escape
Not, half doing what needs to be done
Truthfully, swiftly, rendering apologies when necessary
Ingesting God's Word, daily, as routinely as you prepare for work
Wondering what the Lord would have you to do
In each and every situation, then acting accordingly
Realizing that you are being perfected, moment by moment
That really tuning-in to the Lord, takes a great deal of fine-tuning
Ignoring people and things which create nothing but static, interference
Holding onto His love, not bargaining it away, ever again
Realizing that He, alone, is your only true friend
Wanting, only, more of Him and letting nothing get in the way
Knowing that He always has time to listen, to anything that you say
Drawing near to His bosom seeking comfort and love
Allowing Him to wash you clean, daily, while renewing your faith
Allowing Him to direct your steps, laying out the path that you must take

Leaving those things behind as He so directs
Grasping, cleaving desperately to His outstretched hand
Wanting, in your singleness, your oneness, to be one with Him
To love Him with all of your heart, desiring to please only Him
Knowing that, Father God will determine right from wrong
For in pleasing Him, you will have sealed your fate
Eternal life with Jesus, secure in His divine resting place

September 16, 1996 – Monday
(From The Book – Speaking In The Light)

Michelle Louise Pierre

INTIMACY WITHOUT TOUCH

Psalm 16: 5 – 7
The LORD is the portion of mine inheritance and of my cup: thou maintainest my lot.
The lines are fallen unto me in pleasant places ; yea, I have a goodly heritage.
I will bless the LORD, who hath given me counsel:
my reins also instruct me in the night seasons.

Sitting here, in front of this computer monitor as my hands move swiftly
over the keys, trying to capture words that are flitting through my mind,
like the humming bird I just saw with wings rapidly flapping in the breeze.
"LORD, You are awesome!", and I can never say that enough; for, the meaning
of those words grow proportionally day by day, when I look back on what
You have so graciously done for me as sweetly as You please.

Precious LORD, with all of those miracles and blessed saves along this way,
that is my life's journey, I could never have imaged, this time last year, when
my life was in such turmoil, that I would be settled so solidly, right here.
At that time, I could only take it moment by moment, praying that my
sanity would not permanently escape me, while grasping even more tightly,
and at times tenuously, to those things You had taught me to hold dear.

LORD, without Your sovereign love and mercy, I would surely have lost
my mind or committed some act that would have landed me in jail,
then regretting my actions, with so much of time on my hands.
But, oh blessed LORD, You stepped in and stayed with me, through
that dark time, reminding me whose child I actually was, and that I was
better than what I had allowed into my life, while outside of Your plan.

Once I came back to myself, I could finally grasp the need to truly let go
of a relationship and a man, who was trying to pull me off course,
to land me squarely outside of Your blessed will for my life.
In the letting go, I felt more alone than ever, but You ministered to my heart,
rekindling within me new hope that Your former promises still were
"Yea" and "Amen", and I would one day be another man's wife.

The day is almost approaching, again, and I humbly anticipate all of the good
love that will pour forth from my future husband, because, he too, will
have weathered storms by realizing that You love him very much.
LORD, thank You for teaching us, both, that we would never have been able
to share the level of godly intimacy of the soul, before marriage, with one another,
had we not learned that it is not contingent upon the physicality of sexual touch.

October 21, 2006 – Saturday

INTO YOUR ARMS

Proverbs 31: 11 & 12
The heart of her husband doth safely trust in her,
so that he shall have no need of spoil.
She will do him good and
not evil all the days of her life.

Dear Lord, send me
a man, who loves You
and Your Word, above
fortune and fame.
May he truly delight in
knowing that miracles
still happen, when he calls
upon Your holy name.

Dear Lord, birth in his
heart the capacity to
contain love, faith and
trust beyond measure.
May he see these
three things as much
more precious than
any earthly treasure.

Dear Lord, heal his
mind, and mend the
broken places in
his heart and soul.
May he learn to run
straight into Your
arms and allow
You, him, to hold.

In Jesus' blessed name!!!
Thank You and Amen!!!

March 3, 2001 – Saturday

Michelle Louise Pierre

IT'S OKAY TO LOVE, AGAIN

Psalm 22: 10
I was cast upon thee from the womb:
thou art my God from my mother's belly.

Jeremiah 1: 5
Before I formed thee in the belly I knew thee;
and before thou camest forth out of the
womb I sanctified thee, and I ordained
thee a prophet unto the nations.

My son, My daughter, it is okay
to love, again, for this is the one,
whom I have sent to you.
This is the one, with whom all
of the dreams I have given you,
will be manifested and come true.

They, alone, hold the love in
their heart, that will unlock that
secret place reserved just for them.
You can relax in their love, for
it was refined in the furnace of
affliction, while touching My hem.

This is a love that was birthed
in heaven, even before time,
as you knew it, could begin.
Pray, always, for them to stay
under My divine protection,
choosing to abstain from sin.

You, two, must never forget
that the weapons of your warfare
are not formed in carnality.
They must instead proceed from
My throne, being mighty to pull
down strongholds, for eternity.

You are to be soul winners for
My Kingdom, for I have chosen you,
long before you chose Me.
Know this, the sifting process will
begin, anew, but it is for your ultimate
good, in line with your glorious destiny.

In A Solitary Way

You were created to set this
world on fire as you, together,
snatch souls from hell's flame.
You are chosen, you are blessed,
you are loved, you will lead others
to call upon My Son, Jesus', holy name!

I will lead you by My Spirit as long as
you, both, keep your hands from
succumbing to iniquity of any kind.
Be strong for each other, so you will,
one day, ebb and flow as a holy couple,
one in body, soul and mind.

July 18, 2006 – Tuesday

Michelle Louise Pierre

JUST BETWEEN US

Psalm 121: 1 – 3
I will lift up mine eyes unto the hills, from whence cometh my help.
My help cometh from the LORD, which made heaven and earth.
He will not suffer thy foot to be moved: he that keepeth thee will not slumber.

Sitting here on my living
room sofa, preparing to do
a video workout, as thoughts
of You, still my mind.
I am so grateful to You, LORD,
for You have loosed the
shackles that were once firmly
linked, and had me in such a bind.

This level of freedom is new to me,
and when I think on where, and
what manner of man, You in Your
sovereignty, just delivered me from.
My contented heart, comforted
by Your touch of redemption,
renewal and restoration, can
continue its steady, rhythmic hum.

Father God, thank You, once
again, for sweet rescue when
I was broken, repentant and
crying out to You, in dire need.
For You, alone, saved me from
choices that would have been,
if brought to fruition, akin to
living out hell on earth, indeed.

Father, Son and Holy Spirit, continue
to rest, rule and abide in my heart,
bringing grace and mercy, while
building unshakeable, faith-filled trust.
For, it is in moments such as these,
that being single brings such peace, as I,
uninterruptedly, bathe in this intimate
moment of love, just between us.

Thank You, LORD,
Amen and Amen!

February 16, 2006 – Thursday

In A Solitary Way

JUST THE TOUCH

Isaiah 55: 8 & 9
For my thoughts are not your thoughts,
neither are your ways my ways, saith the LORD.
For as the heavens are higher than the earth,
so are my ways higher than your ways,
and my thoughts than your thoughts.

Dear LORD, touch my future husband, right now,
in the name of Jesus, Your Only Begotten Son!
We need Your divine intervention, to clear the pathways,
while removing all obstacles to us becoming one.

We need You, LORD, more than ever as we prepare
to discuss, in earnest, what our next step must be.
We know You put us together and that, as a godly
couple, we are being called to fulfill our destiny.

Be in the midst of our separate lives right now,
teaching us when to say, "Yes!" and when to say "No!"
Continue to order our steps, Dear LORD, as we place our
hands in Yours, trusting You to teach us which way to go.

Forgive us of our sins, known and unknown, cleansing our hearts from
all unrighteousness, as we surrender in humble submission to You.
Father God, we stand in awe of Your greatness, while blessing Your
holy name, for all that You have already brought us through.

Continue to lead, guide and protect us, while showing us what we must
do, to walk together in holiness, according to Your sovereign plan.
Dear LORD, thank You, as always, for intervening so miraculously in
our lives, with just the touch of Your loving, gracious omnipotent hand.

In Jesus' holy name, we pray! Amen!

October 21, 2006 – Saturday

Michelle Louise Pierre

KNIT TOGETHER BY GOD

Genesis 2: 21 – 24
And the LORD God caused a deep sleep to fall upon Adam, and he slept:
and he took one of his ribs, and closed up the flesh instead thereof; And the rib,
which the LORD God had taken from man, made he a woman, and brought her unto
the man. And Adam said, This is now bone of my bones, and flesh of my flesh:
she shall be called Woman, because she was taken out of Man.
Therefore shall a man leave his father and his mother,
and shall cleave unto his wife: and they shall be one flesh.

Honey, a moment in your arms, I know would be
to me like a warm, soothing, refreshing, healing balm.
To lie there with you, allowing my mind to freely roam,
while basking in your manly essence, stilling and calm.

I will love you more than my own life, second only to our LORD,
desiring to forever and always do you good and not harm.
I think of our future together, ministering and falling more and more
in love with each other, daily, while walking through life, arm in arm.

We will be praying and studying God's Word together, going well
beyond the realm either of us was meant to achieve, on our own.
We will know instinctively that we were predestined to be together, at
such a time as this, for I am flesh of your flesh, bone of your bone.

Your God is my God, and the love that He is nurturing within us,
is drawing us closer and closer to meeting, with each passing new day.
The LORD created us for each other, and we have been living parallel
lives, that He will, one day, choose to intersect, in His own special way.

If necessary, I know that you would lay down your life for me, and I, for you;
for, this is the bond of love, that the LORD intended for us, from the start.
Dear LORD, we will be eternally grateful to You for reuniting us, for we know
that it is Your righteousness, not ours, that has knit together our hearts.

***Blessed be the name of the LORD!!!**$

October 21, 2006 – Saturday

In A Solitary Way

LITTLE GIRL, I LOVE YOU

Psalm 115: 11 - 15
Ye that fear the LORD, trust in the LORD: he is their help and their shield.
The LORD hath been mindful of us: he will bless us; he will bless the house of
Israel; he will bless the house of Aaron. He will bless them that fear the LORD,
both small and great. The LORD shall increase you more and more, you and
your children. Ye are blessed of the LORD which made heaven and earth.

Psalm 129: 2
Many a time have they afflicted me from my youth:
yet they have not prevailed against me.

Girl child born
Lying in a crib, in a darkened room, all alone
What thoughts go through your innocent, baby mind
I cannot know
I can, however, feel the fear that is gripping your heart
I know the loneliness you felt, even then
I reach down and pick you up
I cradle you to my bosom
I calm your fears
With the touch of human arms
I pull that comforting thumb from your mouth
Praying for the Lord
To be your comfort and strength
I rock you back and forth
Putting you back into bed, only
When you are peacefully asleep
Know this little girl, I love you

Girl child now three years old
Rocking away on a horse with springs
Rocking, rocking to soothe her fears
Rocking in a darkened vestibule, all alone
Going nowhere fast
Determination etched in your baby face
I take you from your rocker
Cradling you in my arms as instructed by God
I pray for peace to dwell in your heart
I pray for you to feel
What is in my heart for you
Your own heart learning to accept
What I have come to share
You recline peacefully
Head on my shoulder
Know this, little girl, I love you

Michelle Louise Pierre

Girl child now seven years old
Night terrors plague your immature mind
Parents try to soothe
It simply cannot stop the pounding of your young heart
They place you beside them of their bed
Turning back to each other
You lay there, seeing demonic shadows on the wall
Quietly terrified, so as not to disturb their peace
Later on, fear overwhelming you
Covering you with sweat
You cry out
Now, they place you between them
Taking out their Bible
Daddy reads you to sleep
The sun comes up
Finally awakening
The incident is "hushed up"
Leaving you confused
Dealing with issues that are way out of your realm

Later down the road, alone under your bed
The only place, where you feel safe
"Boney" child's arms encircling your body
Chanting to yourself
Believing the lies of the enemy
"No more love left for you"
I step into the room
I pull you gently from under that bed
Breaking the rhythm of deception's, deadly song
I enfold you in my arms
Calming you
Telling you that all will be all right
The tension leaves your body
Hope quickens your heartbeat
The Lord has sent me to comfort you, deep within
Know this, little girl, I love you

Girl child, now twelve years old
Rejected, battered, molested and abused
Emotionally wrecked
Allowed to speak about it for a short time
Not allowed to heal
Situation pushed down so deeply
The screams can no longer be heard
Nightmares become a nightly routine
Yet, you keep it to yourself
Trying to feel safe
Not ever, really knowing how

In A Solitary Way

I see you there little girl
I reach out my hand to you
Exuding all of the positive affection that I have for you
You tremble, fearful of reaching beyond your "space"
Not knowing if, I am simply the next in line to hurt you
Innocence, not completely shattered
Coming out of your corner to grasp my hand
I look into your almost black, beautiful eyes
I see the hurt, the pain, the fear
I cry for you
With you
I hug you as close as my own skin will allow
I have come, stronger, healthier
To dry up all of your tears
I am adult, strengthened from within
Fortified by the touch of my omnipotent Father's loving hand

Now, we are skipping in the sunshine
Twirling, twirling, laughing with joy
Surrounded by the Son's holy, loving light

Never forget
I am you
Dear little girl
And
I love you!

November 8, 1997 – Sunday
(From the Book – The God Of All Comfort)

Michelle Louise Pierre

LIVING SINGLE, GLORIOUSLY!

I will not bow my head down.
I will not feel second class or ashamed.
I am single and living for the Lord.
I have been saved and renamed.

He now calls me His blessed child.
He has called me to this season.
He is all knowing and in charge.
He doesn't owe me a reason.

I do owe Him praise, for as long as I live.
I will surrender my flesh, under His authority.
I will study His Word, to show myself approved.
I will proclaim His name, going against the majority.

Righteousness is found in submission to Christ.
Holiness must be my all-consuming desire.
Purity in mind and body, not just a notion.
Purge me oh Lord, with Your baptism of fire.

The Father must get the glory out of my life.
Jesus fought that battle through obedience, victoriously.
Teach me obedience, beyond the tugs of my flesh.
Now, I am free, whole, and living single, gloriously!

October 31, 2001 – Wednesday

In A Solitary Way

LORD, AT WHAT PRICE THIS BLESSING?

Revelation 7: 9 – 14 & 17
After this I beheld, and, lo, a great multitude, which no man could number, of all nations,
and kindreds, and people, and tongues, stood before the throne, and before the Lamb, clothed with
white robes, and palms in their hands; And cried with a loud voice, saying, Salvation to our God which
sitteth upon the throne, and unto the Lamb. And all the angels stood round about the throne, and about
the elders and the four beasts, and fell before the throne on their faces, and worshipped God, Saying, Amen:
Blessing, and glory, and wisdom, and thanksgiving, and honour, and power, and might, be unto our God for ever
and ever. Amen. And one of the elders answered, saying unto me, What are these which are arrayed in white robes?
and whence came they? And I said unto him, Sir, thou knowest. And he said to me, These are they which came
out of great tribulation, and have washed their robes, and made them white in the blood of the Lamb.
…For the Lamb which is in the midst of the throne shall feed them, and shall lead them
unto living fountains of waters: and God shall wipe away all tears from their eyes.

Casting out demons in the name of the Lord.
Granted power from on high, stronger than any cord.

Will not be broken, unless it is at His omnipotent hands.
God has chosen me, and you, to execute His plans.

Loneliness envelops your heart like a shroud.
Others simply look at you, like you are acting too proud.

Coming home, alone, to mull over what just went on.
Looking out the patio door, quietly, trying to calm the inner storm.

This storm, is brewing, because you have to answer His call.
Time out for playing church; He is calling you to get on the ball.

Square your shoulders and say, "Yes.", to the task that lies at your feet.
This is not the time to think about running, or to think of beating a hasty retreat.

Sure, sacrifices have been made, and will continue to be made, for His sake.
You cannot grow a beautiful garden, without using a hoe and a rake.

The soil needs to be tilled, just like you need to be put through the paces.
How else can you know, without a doubt, that you will be there at the end of the races?

Friendships come and go, leaving little areas of discontent in your heart.
Wanting to close off from the world, and from the pain, no longer be an active part.

Still, His call is strong and He will not leave you comfortless, or in harm's way.
He will continue to draw those, whom He needs for you, to kneel down and pray.

Lord, at what price this blessing of intercession, deliverance and sharing Your healing touch?
You ask this, in all sincerity, because you did not fully realize the cost would be so much.

At times, being mocked because of the level of commitment that you have to the Lord.
Engaging in conversations with other Christians, whose eyes glaze over, looking bored.

When mentioning relationships, especially between male and female, their eyes light right up.
Walking away, wondering if they will ever come to the saving knowledge of what is in His cup.

They prefer to think of the cup of joy, but that cup is not just all things lovely and of great cheer.
The Lord, Jesus, Himself, at the thought of drinking from that cup, sweat blood like tears.

Jesus, is our example and I must go in the direction that our Father is pointing out.
We can no longer afford to turn to the right or the left, this is not a boxing match or a bout.

There is a war in the spirit realm, over our soul's final destination; we have to learn this lesson.
Can you say, "No matter what Lord, use me; I am willing to pay the price for this blessing."?

April 17, 2000 – Monday

In A Solitary Way

LOVE, FROM YOUR VALENTINE'S HEART

Psalm 51: 10
Create in me a clean heart, O God; and renew a right spirit within me.

Sitting here at my desk, thinking on the goodness of the Lord, while
cheerfully saying, "Happy Valentine's Day", to all of my young students,
with their eyes beaming so brightly, full of such sweet innocence.
Fully knowing, that even though I am still single, this day used to be one
anticipated with a longing and a dread so deep, it would leave me
feeling paralyzed, or in the very least, cranky and tense.

But, You, Dear Lord, have come into my heart and forgiven me
for things done foolishly, as I let my lonely heart, time and again,
dictate to me remedies only meant to be temporary, at best.
Dear Lord, thank You, for giving me Your peace that surpasses
even my own understanding, for surely within human consideration,
I should be depressed and feeling, more than a bit, hopeless.

Now, I look at the cute, little, red teddy bear given to me by one of my
students, this morning, along with a card and a sweet, delicious, red
sucker attached, with a fourth grader's printing scribbled on it.
To me, this is Your way of telling me, to be grateful for the small things in
life, for out of them, come blessings that wrap firmly around the soul,
warmly breathing new life into the fertile soil, of a humbled spirit.

I am so grateful to You, my sweet Jesus; I just want to cry, for You,
alone, have mended this heart, and also given to me a new song to sing,
as melodies and verses poetically collide, one after another, within my soul.
Blessed be Your holy and wondrous name, Lord, for taking what was once
so broken, by the stinging, cold bitterness of deception, as in my repentance,
You, wonderful Savior, have completely restored me, making me whole.

That is why this single valentine's heart has made the conscious choice, above
all else, to give You praise for the comfort of the Holy Spirit's tender ministrations,
that make me want to get up out of my office chair and dance, right in this place.
Heavenly Father, thank You, for knowing me before I was formed in my
mother's womb, and for placing this hunger and thirst in my heart, that can be
fed and quenched by no other, except by Your unconditional love, mercy and grace.

February 14, 2006 – Tuesday

Michelle Louise Pierre

MERE WORDS

Psalm 42: 1 & 2
As the hart panteth after the water brooks,
so panteth my soul after thee, O God.
My soul thirsteth for God, for the living God:
when shall I come and appear before God?

Dear LORD, Savior of my soul, mere words
will never be able to fully express to You in a
tangible way, just how much I love and adore You.
I do not even want to think about what my life would
be like without You, and I am so very grateful that we, my
future husband and I, both, give You the honor, You are due.

For if, our very soul's survival, had not been a part
of Your divine plan, we would surely never meet,
one day, and fall deeply in love with one another.
With each passing day, You create within our hearts
our own songs of love, with music tuned only to ears,
that are humbled in Christ, first, as sister and brother.

Loving You, Dear LORD, has made me want to be a
better woman, so that I can be the wife and helpmeet
he will need to minister Your grace, upon this earth.
LORD, You have truly brought us both from a mighty
long way and have judged us faithful, covered in the blood
of Your Son, Jesus, in whom we have this glorious new birth!

Dear Heavenly Father, mere words will never be able to express the
gratitude that we feel at Your blessing us with the miracles that can
only be found in this covenant relationship, with Jesus, Your Son.
Dear Lord, continue to strengthen us in our inner man, as we patiently and
diligently continue the work You have given us in this our single season,
fighting all battles head on, in Your grace, until victory is won!

July 18, 2006 – Tuesday

MY STRENGTH, MY SONG, MY SALVATION

Isaiah 12: 1 & 2
And in that day thou shalt say, O LORD, I will praise thee: though thou wast angry with me, thine anger is turned away, and thou comfortedst me. Behold, God is my salvation; I will trust, and not be afraid: for the LORD JEHOVAH is my strength and my song; he also is become my salvation.

Wearied from fighting a fight, that should not
have been mine, alone, in the first place.
Trying to save a relationship that was ending
in what initially stung, and felt like a disgrace.

Hearing You speak to my heart, bringing comfort to
my soul, in knowing that this is what must be done.
For to live holy is not a suggestion, but a command,
lived out for our edification by Jesus, Your Son.

Reading Your Word as Isaiah, twelfth chapter, verses
one and two washed over my soul, caused joy to well up.
Bringing with that joy, realization that even though I had gone astray,
in repentance, You had forgiven me and was now refilling my cup.

Lord, how wondrous and marvelous is Your name,
worthy to be praised from mountain tops and our valleys low.
Thank You, LORD JEHOVAH, for using what the enemy had intended
for our destruction, to instead cause us in You, to further mature and grow.

Thank You, Jesus, for restoring our time of fellowship, where
I was no longer trying to get You to go along with me for the ride.
Thank You, for revealing to me that truly letting go of him, was indeed
the right course of action, regardless of the tugging of my fleshly pride.

Lord, I pray Your blessing on both of us, as we begin anew on this
straight and narrow way, without second thought or hesitation.
For I know that You will surely do for him, what You have done for me, by
reminding him, that You, too, are his Strength, his Song and his Salvation.

November 11, 2005 – Friday

Michelle Louise Pierre

MY VALENTINE'S HEART

Lamentations 3: 19 – 25
Remembering mine affliction and my misery, the wormwood and the gall.
My soul hath them still in remembrance, and is humbled in me.
This I recall to my mind, therefore have I hope. It is of the LORD'S
mercies that we are not consumed, because his compassions fail not.
They are new every morning: great is thy faithfulness.
The LORD is my portion, saith my soul; therefore will I hope in him.
The LORD is good unto them that wait for him, to the soul that seeketh him.

Reaching, grasping, falling, then feeling Your arms around me
pulling me up, as I fall in love with You, over and over, again.
Going this way and that, searching for human love and friendship,
with other lonely hearts, lost hopelessly in their own pain and sin.

Getting sick and tired of feeling that something was missing from my life,
year after year, as a single woman, whose faith, at times, would waver.
Still, holding onto the divine promises that You made me in those times
of loneliness, as I was enveloped, time and again, in Your divine favor.

Finally coming to the conclusion that Your steadfast love is the only true
love, that I will ever really be able to depend on, to never leave nor forsake.
For that kind of undying, devoted love was kindled in the flames of obedience,
that took You straight to Calvary to die, and be raised up again, for our sake.

Lord, You just did something very special for me and the person, Tonya,
whom You used to do it, will never really know how much that gesture meant.
I just checked my e-mail, as I was feeling a bit down being alone, again, on this day
designed for couples, only to find a beautiful e-card that she, a married friend, had sent.

Lord, thank You for reminding me that You love me with an everlasting love that is
always thinking of me, and is one I can forever depend on to never hurt me, or depart.
You, alone, sweet Jesus, have taught me, and keep teaching me, how to love and how to
receive that perfect love from You – Happy Valentine's Day, Lord, my valentine's heart.

February 14, 2004 – Saturday

In A Solitary Way

NEVER ANY SLACK

Psalm 45: 1
My heart is inditing a good matter:
I speak of the things which
I have made touching the king:
my tongue is the pen of a ready writer.

God, I love You more and more each day, as praise psalms, songs
pour forth from my heart, flowing down to paper from pen.
Lord, gratitude is what I feel, but hardly comes close
to what is really there, for that I can hardly comprehend.

I have found that in the midst of this agape love, You have expanded my heart
to deeper depths, the very existence of, were before untapped and unknown.
I have attempted to live a life consecrated solely to You, for many years, praying
to one day be gifted with a compassionate, passionate, loving man of my own.

In so doing, You are letting he and I know that it is okay to love, again,
and cleave to each other, while desiring from each other, never to roam.
You are the One responsible for sealing our hearts together in the Spirit,
before we would even meet, and find in each other, our center, our home.

Warm, soothing thoughts now flow, wondrously through my mind,
when I think about the day, we will become one, in every way.
Lord, continue this humbling, solitary journey of self-discovery, within us,
as this healing in our inward parts, the results of which, You will openly display.

When the time comes for us to more tangibly express our love for each other,
I want us to let the floodgates open, fully, letting go completely, no holding back.
LORD, then continually anoint, restore, refill and revive us, for what lies ahead
of us, day by day, as we function as one, so there is between us, never any slack.

May 13, 2004 – Thursday

Michelle Louise Pierre

NIGHT SONG

Psalm 42: 8
Yet the LORD will command his
lovingkindness in the daytime,
and in the night his song shall be with me,
and my prayer unto the God of my life.

Night after night, spent alone with no one,
Dear LORD, to comfort me, but You.
Wondering, if the dream of marriage and
family, will ever really come true.

Yet, knowing in my heart of hearts, that Your
promises to me are "Yea" and "Amen".
Fighting the urge to give up, by holding on
to other solitary times, remembering when.

I call to remembrance the times of sweet rescue
and times of miracles dispensed just for me.
I bask in Your love, renewed, restored and
revived as I am tenderly ministered to by Thee.

Dear Heavenly Father, thank You, for the gift of
Your Son, Jesus, who in turn, left us the Holy Ghost.
For, the comfort now surging within me, comes directly
from Him, this morning at 2:05 AM, on the West Coast.

I wholeheartedly say blessed be Your holy and wondrous name, as praising and
worshipping You, again surge through me, reminding me to Whom I really belong.
Contented, I lovingly place my soul in Your tender care, on my way back to sleep, Dear
LORD, grateful indeed, as within my heart, again, beats our triumphant night song.

October 10, 2006 – Saturday

In A Solitary Way

NO MATTER WHAT IT LOOKS LIKE

2 Corinthians 1: 20 – 22
For all the promises of God in him are yea, and in him Amen,
unto the glory of God by us. Now he which stablisheth us with you
in Christ, and hath anointed us, is God; Who hath also sealed us,
and given the earnest of the Spirit in our hearts.

No matter what it looks like,
God is still very much on the throne.
The LORD is in full control, and He has
promised never to leave you alone.

No matter what it looks like, God told
you not to bend your knee to any man.
The LORD has done too much for you
to crumble, you must continue to stand.

No matter what it looks like, God's
arms are around you keeping you still.
The LORD will bring comfort to your
broken heart; get back in the circle of His will.

No matter what it looks like, God's
promises are still, "Yea" and "Amen".
The LORD is telling you to get it together, lean
fully on Him, and start flying straight again.

December 19, 2005 – Monday

Michelle Louise Pierre

NOT MAN ENOUGH FOR ME

John 3: 19 – 21
As many as I love, I rebuke and chasten: be zealous therefore, and repent.
Behold, I stand at the door, and knock: if any man hear my voice, and open the door,
I will come in to him, and will sup with him, and he with me. To him that overcometh will I grant
to sit with me in my throne, even as I also overcame, and am set down with my Father in his throne.

Fight for your soul's salvation; not giving up, or in,
until the totality of sweet victory, Jesus allows you to see.
For I can pledge my heart to no one less than God's best, which
means, if you will not, cannot do this, you are not man enough for me.

If you choose, in the face of a new, blessed chance
at contented love and happiness, to run and hide.
If you have allowed your fears, to cause you
not to draw strength from Jesus' bleeding side.

If you would rather stay in the dark, where you feel safe,
protected from the world, hiding behind a rock or a tree.
Then, according to what the Lord has envisioned,
you are not man enough for me.

Father will not allow me to fall back on my desire for you,
to cloud my judgment, in the face of what I have seen.
For, He has shown me that He is preparing me, like Esther,
to be wed to the man, to whom I will be called queen.

So, if you will not fight with all that is within,
to be delivered and set completely free.
Then, I am truly sorry, my brother,
but you are not man enough for me.

I fight the good fight, alone, now, for this is my season of singleness
and the joy and comfort it affords, no one will ever be able to take away.
I am, now, in the process of preparation, as are His other children;
the ones, who have allowed Him total access, when they kneel to pray.

My friend and brother, reach out to Jesus, while you still can and His glory is right there;
before the earthly curtain is drawn on you, and you arrive at your destination in eternity.
Don't do it because I am asking, for you know that I cannot save your soul; but, only
in the doing, the Lord has told me, tonight, you will then be man enough for me.

May 23, 2000 – Tuesday

In A Solitary Way

NOT WITHOUT JESUS!

Joshua 24: 13 - 15
And I have given you a land for which ye did not labour, and cities which ye built not, and ye dwell in them; of the vineyards and oliveyards which ye planted not do ye eat. Now therefore fear the LORD, and serve him in sincerity and in truth: and put away the gods which your fathers served on the other side of the flood, and in Egypt; and serve ye the LORD. And if it seem evil unto you to serve the LORD, choose you this day whom ye will serve; whether the gods which your fathers served that were on the other side of the flood, or the gods of the Amorites, in whose land ye dwell: but as for me and my house, we will serve the LORD.

Dear LORD, You know that I am
awaiting the blessing of a mate of my own.
The one after Your own heart, from whom You
promised, my heart would never want to roam.

I am finding that those, who show interest, are simply
looking at the exterior and wanting to pounce.
I no longer give them the time of day, because in their
character I don't see You, my Jesus, not one ounce.

LORD, help me to stay strong as in this single season
of my life, I continue to offer up to You, my best.
Help me to say, "No, thank you!" to all, whom the enemy
will try to clothe in sheep's clothing to, my soul, test.

I have to keep my mind stayed on Thee, while
keeping my eyes opened to discern their real intent.
Holy Spirit, thank You, for continuously prompting my
heart, with blessed, wise counsel that is heaven sent.

I am to look for a man, who has a servant's heart, to whom
"What Would Jesus Do!" is more than just a cute saying.
He needs to lead a lifestyle, in line with Your Word, and when
he falls short, goes immediately to repentance and praying.

LORD, You keep prompting me with a phrase that sums this all up,
for I can no longer look for those things to merely consume on my lust.
This brother is going to be uniquely set apart, just for me, and he will
be looking for a woman, whose lifestyle, too, is lived – "Not without Jesus!"

February 25, 2006 – Saturday

Michelle Louise Pierre

ONE PLUS ONE

EQUALS ONE

Genesis 2:24
Therefore shall a man leave his father and his mother,
and shall cleave unto his wife: and they shall be one flesh.

Matthew 19: 5 & 6
And said, For this cause shall a man leave father and mother,
and shall cleave to his wife: and they twain shall be one flesh?
Wherefore they are no more twain, but one flesh.
What therefore God hath joined together,
let not man put asunder.

One plus one equals one
In the Kingdom of God
For He explicitly said
The two shall become one flesh

As you stand, hand in hand, before the Lord today
Proclaiming your undying love for one another
Do not forget that God must fit into this equation
He, after all, can be considered
The plus and the equal signs

It is He, who will seal you together
It is He, who will determine your equality
It is He, who will lead you to your knees
It is He, who will command the blessings
It is He, who will be the controlling force

May the love that you feel this day
Include a place of priority for
The Father, the Son and the Holy Ghost
May the love that you feel this day
Include a place of priority for your new spouse
May the love that you feel this day
Include a place of priority for yourself
And, God willing, may the love that you feel this day
One day, include a place of priority for your children

May you be given the godly wisdom
That will be needed
To determine the proper placement
Of each one of those loves

In A Solitary Way

They seem separate, but are one
For they are all a part of you
Your innate capacity to give and receive love
For your Creator is love
You are made in His image

Know that in order to be a complete one
In this final equation
You will need to be a complete one
In and of yourself, in solitude
No props, no crutches, no excuses
Divinely healed from the inside, out

You must already have learned how to be content, alone
With no one to entertain you, but yourself

You must already have learned to put a smile on your own face
When you think of how much you love you

You must already have learned how to "get a prayer through"
On your own behalf as well as on the behalf of others

You must already have learned how to deeply love, trust
And completely lean only on the Lord

You must already have learned to read
The Word of God daily, and seek His divine face

Through all of this
You will have learned that He created you whole

For, when he or she fell in love with you
They were not given the assignment
Of keeping you from fragmenting
Into a million pieces
They are not your "super glue"

You must come into this relationship in solid form
In right standing with the Lord
Sanctified, satisfied, ego intact

Then when friction does arise
It will not come from the rubbing together
Of two broken, incomplete people

It will come from the attempt
To meld together two separate, whole individuals
Into one synchronized, harmonic life

Michelle Louise Pierre

May the melody of the music
That your love will make together
As you graciously proceed on
With the rest of your newly joined lives
Be filled with the variety of notes and tones
That will make up your personal symphony
The highs, the mediums and the lows

May you, both, firmly realize that God is the only conductor
Leave the baton in His, more than capable, hands

May God bless your holy union
With His love, grace, wisdom and mercy

From this day forward
One plus one equals one

August 29, 1996 - Thursday
(From The Book – Speaking In The Light)

In A Solitary Way

ONLY THE LORD!

Jeremiah 17:14
Heal me, O LORD, and I shall be healed;
save me, and I shall be saved:
for thou art my praise

John 15: 1 – 4
I am the true vine, and my Father is the husbandman. Every branch in me that
beareth not fruit he taketh away: and every branch that beareth fruit, he purgeth it,
that it may bring forth more fruit. Now ye are clean through the word
which I have spoken unto you. Abide in me, and I in you.

Only the Lord could have answered the prayers of
two of His wounded children, now set free and healed,
as He brought us together at the same time and place.
He is the only one, who could have orchestrated
that so flawlessly, as we went through our separate,
single lives, being purged by His loving grace.

May the anointing over our individual lives,
grow stronger day by day, until we are
united in the eyes of God and man, as one.
May the blood of Jesus protect and keep us
safe, as we go about our daily tasks, being
led by the Spirit as a daughter and son.

Only the Lord could have seen into the
depths of our very souls, and known that we
would be for each other, a perfect match.
He is the One, who closed doors on previous
relationships, and when the time came for us
to meet, completely threw open the door's latch.

We serve an awesome God, who loves us beyond
what eye could see, hand could hold, finite mind
could left alone imagine, or bring into existence.
Our Father's love has swept over us, continuously
cleansing us along the way, as we surrender our hearts
to one another, no longer with any need for resistance.

October 21, 2006 – Saturday

Michelle Louise Pierre

OPENED MY HEART TO LOVE, AGAIN

Isaiah 40: 31
But they that wait upon the LORD shall renew their strength;
they shall mount up with wings as eagles; they shall run,
and not be weary; and they shall walk, and not faint.

Dear Lord, I woke up this morning knowing that
something quite different is going on inside me, now.
Been celibate and single for a great many years,
in fasting and humbling my soul to You, I still bow.

You, alone, gave me the strength to hang on,
even when doubt and shame tried to cover my head.
You, were the one, who told me that I was Your
child, and this flesh I had to render to You, as dead.

In the yielding, You tenderly and subtly mended all
of the hurts and wounds from my weary, troubled past.
You are now settling the old scores, that threatened
to consume my life in obscurity, at long last.

Like a phoenix rising from the ashes, You have
taken an old, buried feeling, and made it quite new.
Realizing that I have never loved a man, as You intended,
for this could only be obtained by first, truly loving You.

During this time, I have repented, as You and I have
lovingly walked hand and hand, and heart in heart.
There were times, when I would stumble, but You always
assured me that I would never, from Your love, depart.

Lord, to say that I love You, would not adequately express the
deep well of emotion, that floods so sweetly through my soul.
The best thing I have ever done with my life, has been to
submit it to Your leanings, placing in Your hands full control.

I honestly don't know whether this new man in my
life will actually be more than just a very good friend.
Dear Lord, I am trusting You to reveal this to me, in Your
timing, for You have opened my heart to love, again.

September 11, 2002 - Wednesday

PEEPING THROUGH THE GATE

In John 17: 15 – 17, Jesus says,
"I pray not that thou shouldest take them out of the world,
but that thou shouldest keep them from the evil.
They are not of the world, even as I am not of the world.
Sanctify them through thy truth: thy word is truth.
As thou hast sent me into the world,
even so have I also sent them into the world.
And for their sakes I sanctify myself,
that they also might be sanctified through the truth."

Went down the street to the corner store
Just one more thing to do before I see my front door

Salt, pepper, sugar lined up neatly as I cruise by
Stopping briefly to inspect a new brand, shaking my head with a sigh

So many choices, but let's keep it plain
Too many choices could make a person go insane

Minding my own business, strolling down each aisle
Then in comes this brother, looking my way with a beautiful smile

I look even more intently at the products, to help me to focus my mind
Man, oh man, it is much more difficult than I thought, because he is fine

Knowing my status, a child of the King, I cannot afford to misstep
Straightening up my back a little more, walking by with new pep

I return his smile, but leave no room for him to take it further than that
The Lord has to be the One, who makes my decisions now, and that is that

On my mind now: bread, milk, meat and eggs
Lord, have mercy, in those shorts, did You see his legs?

Now, he's changed directions, turning around, going my same way
"Focus, girlfriend!", I can hear that inner voice within me, clearly say

He asks me if he can talk to me, to take up just a few minutes of my time
He leans even closer now, speaking in a low voice, talking with his hands like a mime

As it turns out, he is giving a party, Saturday, and wants me to be his personal guest
I know, I should say, "No" right away, but what could it hurt to listen, more or less

I take his number, as he talks even more seductively, telling him I'll think it over for awhile
He knows that he's got my attention, so now he has added a strut to his smile

Michelle Louise Pierre

Seeing him walk away, lost in the moment, as he zooms off like a rocket
I turn back to the business at hand, sticking his number down in my jeans pocket

Knowing I can do nothing but tear it up later, after I finish my shopping, anyway
I start thinking "You still got it, girl", knowing immediately that is not the right thing to say

Arriving home, having forgotten the note, and the temptation that it came wrapped in
I put away my groceries, listen to gospel music, and then boom, conviction settles in

Grabbing that sheet of paper as if the devil, himself, had left it at my door
I rip it to shreds, repent with every fiber of my being, as the tears begin to pour

Noting how vulnerable I could still be to "a line" presented by smooth, brown skin
How easily I ate up all that attention, blindly heading, willfully right into sin

Praise God that it did not have to go as far as an actual telephone call
Blessed be the name of the Lord, for saving me from myself, keeping me from that fall

Now, I have learned to allow the Holy Ghost to guard the gates of my mind and heart
I am allowing God's love to permeate my soul, cleansing me for a fresh, new start

Temptation comes in many forms, yours may look a lot different than mine
But, whatever form it takes, whether a person or a thing, it could still put you in a bind

Because sin is sin, Dear One, and you have not "arrived", you will always be bait
Without the Lord on our side, we would all be locked out of heaven
Left, peeping through the gate

October 8, 1998 – Thursday
(From The Book – A Pen Of Iron)

In A Solitary Way

PRAY FOR ME

James 5: 14 – 17
Is any sick among you? let him call for the elders of the church;
and let them pray over him, anointing him with oil in the name of the Lord:
And the prayer of faith shall save the sick, and the Lord shall raise him up;
and if he have committed sins they shall be forgiven him. Confess your
faults one to another, and pray one for another, that ye may be healed.
The effectual fervent prayer of a righteous man availeth much.

Dear Friend, pray for me
that I remain faithful to
the Lord's call.

That my focus remain
centered in the Father's will,
not wavering, at all.

Pray for my mind to stay
on Him, ready to spring
into action, without hesitation
.

That I praise and worship God,
in spirit and in truth, with abandon,
not mindful of impending perspiration.
.

Pray for me to walk in
the boldness, given in
the power of Jesus' might.

That I maintain the fortitude
needed to shatter darkness,
with His holy light.

Pray for me to remain in His
peace, when trouble comes
as close as my own skin.

That I immediately rebuke the
works of the enemy, in the name
of Jesus, our Savior and Friend.

Pray for me, when fiery
trials come, that I will
not want to run and hide.

Michelle Louise Pierre

That I will face them, head on,
praying in the Spirit, for my
soul in Jesus to abide.

Pray for me to walk in this season of
singleness, head held high in holiness,
with God's light upon my face.

That I may minister salvation, to the
lost and confused, telling them to
repent and receive God's grace.

Pray for me, when weariness comes,
from fighting this good fight of faith,
at times, battling loneliness, too.

That I may feel the sweet peace
that comes from surrendering
my heart to Jesus, anew.

Thank you!

Pray for me, as I will for you.
In Jesus' holy and righteous name,
Amen.

October 5, 2001 – Friday

In A Solitary Way

__PREDESTINED LOVE!__

Ephesians 1: 3 – 5
Blessed be the God and Father of our Lord Jesus Christ, who hath blessed us
with all spiritual blessings in heavenly places in Christ: According as he hath
chosen us in him before the foundation of the world, that we should be holy
and without blame before him in love: Having predestinated us unto
the adoption of children by Jesus Christ to himself,
according to the good pleasure of his will.

Love, predestined, before time
for either of us, could actually begin.
I desire to find in you, one day,
my best and closest friend.

I sit here now, my darling, with tears perched
on my eyelids as my desire for you swells.
I want to run from this place, announcing to the world
this future promise of love, not in a whisper, but a yell.

For, the LORD has promised that we are going to do great
exploits in the name of His Son, Jesus, whom we both serve.
He will keep us in the center of His holy will, as through
this life, we successfully maneuver every twist and curve.

In the doing of those great exploits, we will have the
comfort that only comes, from resting in each other hearts.
Giving and receiving love from one another to such a
degree, that we lose track on where you end, and I start.

Abba, continue to bless us with a love, that will never cease,
as we humbly allow You to increase in us, day by day.
Then, use us as a precious gift to the nations, while we minister under
the unction of the Holy Spirit, in Jesus' matchless name, we pray.

Amen and Amen!

October 21, 2006 – Saturday

Michelle Louise Pierre

PRODIGAL DAUGHTER

Psalm 116: 1 – 9
I love the LORD, because he hath heard my voice and my supplications.
Because he hath inclined his ear unto me, therefore will I call upon him
as long as I live. The sorrows of death compassed me, and the pains of
hell gat hold upon me: I found trouble and sorrow. Then called I upon
the name of the LORD; O LORD, I beseech thee, deliver my soul.
Gracious is the LORD, and righteous; yea, our God is merciful.
The LORD preserveth the simple: I was brought low, and he helped me.
Return unto thy rest, O my soul; for the LORD hath dealt bountifully with thee.
For thou hast delivered my soul from death, mine eyes from tears, and
my feet from falling. I will walk before the LORD in the land of the living.

Blessed from head to toe,
a child of the Most High God

Speaking His Word, in season
and out, with feet fully shod

Yet, desiring to taste and see
things left on worldly display

Lusting after the illusion of
human love, turning heart away

Taking the precious inheritance
that the Lord had in store

Running, full swing into the
blazing sun, just outside the door

Spending time, money and effort
on things that shimmer and shine

Ignoring the still, small voice,
telling you not your heart to entwine

Eating, drinking, being merry, fornicating,
not caring what consequences lie just ahead

Waking up, one day, almost insane, eating at
the trough of despair, longing to be dead

Then calling to remembrance the blessings received
in the Father's house, rebelliously, left behind

In A Solitary Way

Repenting in submission to God's will, picking
yourself up, as back home, your heart set-off to find

Head down, in filthy rags, returning, expecting a reception
that would be fitting to your former act of treachery

Instead seeing your Father standing there beaming, with a
robe and a ring, speaking lovingly of your divine destiny

LORD, thank You for being there upon my humble return,
and once again, greeting me without condemnation, guilt or shame

Thank You, Abba, for restoring the desire of my heart to live in holiness,
by strengthening me in the power, obtained by calling on Jesus' holy name

**Blessed be the Father, Son and Holy Ghost
In Jesus' wonderful name, thank You and Amen**

February 25, 2006 – Saturday

Michelle Louise Pierre

READY TO BE IN LOVE

Psalm 37: 3 – 5
Trust in the LORD, and do good; so shalt thou dwell in the land,
and verily thou shalt be fed. Delight thyself also in the LORD;
and he shall give thee the desires of thine heart.
Commit thy way unto the LORD;
trust also in him; and
he shall bring it to pass.

I don't know about you,
but I am ready to be in love, again.
Looking for someone,
who will be more than a friend.

You are a nice guy, you really are,
but you are not the man for me.
I desire to feel that I am truly special to
someone, who has made me top priority!

In all of your busyness, I pray that
you find what it is that you seek.
The feelings of love that I could have had for you,
are like a balloon that has sprung an irreparable leak.

Now, I've had plenty of time to mourn the
passing of a love, that was never allowed to be.
Kind of a shame really, you and I might have
been great, surging toward our united destiny.

Farewell for now my dear friend, may the
Lord continue to bless you from above.
I am off and running, you see, because I have
spent far too much time, being ready to be in love.

November 3, 2003 – Monday

In A Solitary Way

RENEW OUR STRENGTH

1 Samuel 30: 3 – 6
So David and his men came to the city, and, behold, it was burned with fire;
and their wives, and their sons, and their daughters, were taken captives.
Then David and the people that were with him lifted up their voice and wept,
until they had no more power to weep. And David's two wives were taken captives,
Ahinoam the Jezreelitess, and Abigail the wife of Nabal the Carmelite. And David
was greatly distressed; for the people spake of stoning him, because the soul of
all the people was grieved, every man for his sons and for his daughters:
but David encouraged himself in the LORD his God.

Psalm 1: 1 – 3
Blessed is the man that walketh not in the counsel of the ungodly, nor standeth in
the way of sinners, nor sitteth in the seat of the scornful. But his delight is in the law
of the LORD; and in his law doth he meditate day and night. And he shall be like
a tree planted by the rivers of water, that bringeth forth his fruit in his season;
his leaf also shall not wither; and whatsoever he doeth shall prosper.

Sitting here, now, with hot tears streaming
down my face, solely focused on how I feel.
I cannot be there for anyone else, right now,
because this pain runs deep and is very real.

Most often, my friends need me to be there to bolster
them up, when the pressures of life weigh them down.
But, when I am in need, I have to stand alone, save for
the LORD, because most of them simply cannot be found.

Dear LORD, we need You to intercede in our midst,
before this relationship truly goes up in smoke.
Help LORD, for the enemy is as a roaring lion, seeking
to devour all that is godly, making this testimony a joke.

Lead us in the way that we must go to continue to pray
through this time of testing, even when we feel like giving up.
Bring us beyond our fleshly desires to take control back of
our lives, humble our hearts as at Your table, we come to sup.

Feed us LORD, until we can unequivocally feel Your loving
strength, abiding within, renewing our souls, breaking all strongholds.
When we sleep, let it be sweet, as we continue to wait and cling,
to Your promises, hidden deeply within our now, weary souls.

November 26, 2004 – Friday

Michelle Louise Pierre

REST IN HOPE

Psalm 16: 6 – 9
The lines are fallen unto me in pleasant places; yea, I have a goodly heritage.
I will bless the LORD, who hath given me counsel: my reins also instruct me in
the night seasons. I have set the LORD always before me: because he is
at my right hand, I shall not be moved. Therefore my heart is glad,
and my glory rejoiceth: my flesh also shall rest in hope.

Bless the LORD, oh dear soul, for Jesus
the Christ, bids you to come ever near.
Father, God, has set all things in order that
have come into your life, year after year.

You are His son or His daughter, and He is
more than capable of keeping His Word.
Not only will He keep it, but it will be manifested
as miraculously as an olive leaf, in the mouth of a bird.

The flood waters of this time in your single season,
may be threatening to overwhelm your heart.
Hold on, Dear One, for this is only temporary,
meant to gather you closer, and set you apart.

So, seek the LORD, while He may be found;
quickly respond, it is Him, knocking at your door.
The lines are fallen and lain out before you, to walk
into the lightness of His love, for evermore.

Now, allow the Holy Spirit to, once again, comfort your lonely soul,
for only bathed in the Father's love, can we victoriously cope.
Let His presence fill the hollows of your innermost, deeply hidden parts,
as you obediently surrender your will to His, and contentedly rest in hope.

October 26, 2006 – Thursday

In A Solitary Way

SHATTERED!

1 John 4: 7 – 11
Beloved, let us love one another: for love is of God; and every one that loveth is born of God, and knoweth God. He that loveth not knoweth not God; for God is love. In this was manifested the love of God toward us, because that God sent his only begotten Son into the world, that we might live through him. Herein is love, not that we loved God, but that he loved us, and sent his Son to be the propitiation for our sins. Beloved, if God so loved us, we ought also to love one another.

Shattered into a million pieces, like a mirror that has accidentally
slipped from your hand, and now lies scattered all over the cold floor.
That is how your heart now feels, because this time when he left,
you knew, in your very soul, that he was not coming back anymore.

You reach out for the pillow where he used to lay his head, hugging it tightly as
you collapse on the bed to rest; yet, fitful, agitated sleep is all that actually comes.
You dream about the good times, the happy times, when you were so in love;
yet, you wake up to the stark reality of a broken marriage that has been left for
you to clean up, like a good meal that has been eaten, all except for the crumbs.

One day rolls into another, as you learn to fully rely upon the strength
of the omnipotent Lord, to help you to navigate as a single person again.
You seek to find the hope that is professed in His Word, even when hopelessness
and fear have such a firm grasp on your mind, you come to realize that being
a couple has most definitely come to a certain, unchangeable end.

Lord, when this first happened, he said that he had to go and explore his
other options; then, seemingly without a care in the world, actually departed.
You could have been rolled up in your bedclothes, right where you
Laid, petrified by lost in mourning for a relationship that actually,
in hindsight, seemed doomed, well before it even got started.

During the marriage, you tried all that you possibly could to hold it together
in your own strength, without tolerating outside interference of any kind.
It was during one of these times, the realization came that you were the only
one in the relationship, who was actually attempting to mend fences, while
"bending over backwards" as you desperately attempted to anticipate and
accommodate whatever was on his selfish, confused, dissatisfied, angry mind.

Father, You speak in Your Word about the fact that, before you
build a house, you need to set a proper and sound foundation.
Oh Lord, what a mess, we both made of Your precious
commandments, holy covenant, institution and creation.

As you look back, you see that your foundation was built on the love of the world
and each other, along with all that you, as a couple, could materially possess.
Little did you know then, that was one of the weakest foundations
you could have chosen; it would sadly not stand up, under marital stress.

So, when the stress came, as it always does,
the foundation, at first, just shook and shifted.
Then, giving more room for Satan, the world and the flesh to
come in, until, off of its very hinges, it was finally, completely lifted.

Oh Father, if it had not been for Your holy intervention, things would have gotten
even more out of control, and you would have both, completely self-destructed.
But, a voice, from your childhood, told you to reach out to Jesus, in prayer,
because in Him, alone, could your life ever be fully, freely entrusted.

That is when you finally decided to give up your "kicking against
the pricks" and let the Lord's divine will for your lives, be done.
The letting go, that felt like giving up, was one of the hardest
things that you have ever had to do, bar none.

• • •

After that time, when people asked about your marriage,
you could only say that you and he as a couple, were no more.
At times, that was even more than you could bare to say, so you simply
refused to answer the telephone, or even go out of your own front door.

Alone with the Lord was where you felt the most comfortable, because that was truly where
you really needed to be, while being bandaged lovingly by the Holy Spirit, from within.
Of course, it did not help when you did finally venture out, and were approached by
so-called, "well-meaning folks", who could not wait to tell you that, divorce is a sin.

They had mistakenly assumed that you had not read the Word of God for yourself,
as you excruciatingly, agonized, most times in secret, over what was really
happening within the confines of your supposedly happy, "perfect couple" home.
They were not there when you would cry out to God to save your marriage,
no matter what you had to take from your spouse, because you wanted
so desperately to stay in His will and not simply allow your mind to,
on worldly concepts of marriage and divorce, freely roam.

• • •

Well God, thank You for being there with me and being so gracious and
merciful to me; for, Your loving forgiveness and direction unceasingly flowed,
within my very weary, beaten down, devastated and worn outer and inner-being.
Thank You, Lord, for refocusing my mind back to You, as You so tenderly delivered
me and brought about my complete healing; while, simultaneously opening,
yet again, my once blinded eyes, to all that truly "needed seeing".

• • •

It still amazes me, and hopefully always will, as to the way that God's Word can speak directly to a "present time" situation, because it is truly as expressed in Ecclesiastes 1: 9, *"The thing that hath been, it is that which shall be; and that which is done is that which shall be done: and there is no new thing under the sun."*
The previous verse came back to me, when I read Proverbs 22: 24 & 25, which warns us, *"Make no friendship with an angry man; and with a furious man thou shalt not go: Lest thou learn his ways, and get a snare to thy soul."* – When I looked at this and truly let it sink into my spirit, I could not help but to realize that not only did I befriend him, I married him; before I could be set-free, I had truly learned "his ways" and could "give as good as I got", which was certainly what the Lord was trying to prevent, by telling us what type of person to shun.

Now that I have finally learned to love myself, I decided to not take another step without Your Holy Spirit, divinely directing and accompanying me along the way. My determination comes from knowing, for myself, by searching the heart of my loving, living Lord, the foundation of solid rock, Jesus Christ, the Person in whom I desire to build my life, hopes and dreams upon and, to never, again, foolishly be led by my flesh to stray.

There are times, even now, when I still long for the life
that I sincerely wish, with all of my heart, could have been.
But, what a wonderful blessing came as a result of letting go
and allowing Jesus to become my true lifelong Shepherd,
Defender and faithful, loyal, lovingly, devoted Best Friend.

Shattered, is no longer the way that I see myself; now, I look at myself
through my Father's eyes as He intended well before my preordained birth.
I see, instead, a healthy woman filled with heavenly life and love, that has
learned, under The Master's divine tutelage, to boldly faces life's challenges,
while absorbing and radiating the holy beauty of His creation, on this earth.

•   •   •

Take heart all, whether male or female, who have also experienced the blindsided devastation of broken promises, vows that were frivolously cast aside, along with numerous rejections and other abuses, that have ultimately resulted in a divorce. God wants you to know, that He has never stopped loving you, as He has oftentimes dried your weeping eyes in the middle of the night, or in the perceptual darkness of the dawning of a new day; for, it plainly states in His Word, He has and will continue to completely forgive you of your repentant sins, so that you, as well, can be restarted on a new, less destructive, more heavenly narrow course.

IN HIS LOVE'S LIGHT

October 5, 1995 – Thursday
(From the Book – Altars of Praise, Worship, Healing & Deliverance)

Michelle Louise Pierre

SINGLE AND SATISFIED

There are those single people, who actually say that they
are happy with most of the choices, they have made in their life.
Divorced or widowed, now, they are convinced that they no longer
feel the need to be, again, someone else's husband or wife.

They have raised their kids, or are still raising them, for the most part,
by themselves; and, although not easy, they and their children all survived.
They are grateful to the LORD and stand firmly in the knowledge that
He, alone, is responsible for keeping them clothed, well fed and alive.

There are times when they have felt like they were both father and mother,
but ultimately were not, for You stationed people in their lives to fulfill that role.
They have expressed sincere thanks to each and every one of them, for pouring
into their lives, making single parenting not have to take such a devastating toll.

Still, there are those, who have had no children, have never been married,
and blessedly go contently through life, not feeling the need for either one.
They enjoy scheduling their own time to do what they please, when they please,
and have uninterrupted, intimate time with Jesus, God's Only Begotten Son.

They have thoroughly embraced the concept that singleness is a blessing, not
some form of a curse, visited on those, who are not "marriage material" anyway.
They thank the LORD for blessing them with the abundant life, and the faculties
of their mind, to express that gratitude for His faithfulness, whenever they pray.

When looking back, they find they have been able to help out many others,
including children, whom they "raised", and along God's pathway, did guide.
Both of these groups learned to rejoice in the LORD, no matter what state they
were in, fully enjoying their walk with Him, heads held high, single and satisfied.

October 26, 2006 – Thursday

In A Solitary Way

SINGLE GLORY

Unmarried, in a crowded
room, standing all alone.
No one special to talk too,
or even call on the telephone.

Running to and fro, busy, in
the midst of which, still bored.
Of what use could you, a single
soul, possibly be to the Lord?

Still, the Lord keeps calling;
will you answer Him, now?
Cast all your burdens upon Him;
let Him show you how.

Jesus truly loves you with an
everlasting love, from on high.
Don't bury your head in the sand,
waiting for a mate to fall from the sky.

Let's be about the Father's business, while
living out this life, that is to be, our story.
Let the Holy Ghost overshadow you, bringing you
through this single season, to even greater glory!

November 1, 2001 – Thursday

Michelle Louise Pierre

SINGLE PRAISE!

Psalms 100: 4
Enter into his gates with thanksgiving,
and into his courts with praise:
be thankful unto him,
and bless his name.

Stand to your feet, and clap your
hands all ye people, give honor
and glory to the King of kings.
Don't let a barren third finger on the
left hand, mute the level of worship that
should, in your voice, outwardly ring.

Our praise must not be contingent
upon our marital status; for, if we cannot
praise and worship Him, now, when?
This freedom we now should be enjoying, for as quietly
as it is kept, is more often envied by those, whom
we would never suspect, friend, foe and/or kin.

So, when you enter His gates, do it with
thanksgiving, going deeper and deeper,
as you then, enter into His courts with praise.
Let your voice be heard in the congregation, full strength,
for Jesus is listening; and, He desires to lift you higher by
those very hands, sans wedding ring, you now raise.

February 16, 2006 – Thursday

In A Solitary Way

SINGLE VALENTINE

Matthew 25: 1 – 10
Then shall the kingdom of heaven be likened unto ten virgins, which took their lamps,
and went forth to meet the bridegroom. And five of them were wise, and five were foolish.
They that were foolish took their lamps, and took no oil with them: But the wise took oil
in their vessels with their lamps. While the bridegroom tarried, they all slumbered and slept.
And at midnight there was a cry made, Behold, the bridegroom cometh; go ye out to meet him.
Then all those virgins arose, and trimmed their lamps. And the foolish said unto the wise, Give us
of your oil; for our lamps are gone out. But the wise answered, saying, Not so; lest there be not enough
for us and you: but go ye rather to them that sell, and buy for yourselves. And while they went to buy,
the bridegroom came; and they that were ready went in with him to the marriage: and the door was shut.

Being single, in what seems like a coupled world can, if you
allow it, bring discouragement to the most stout at heart.
Still, Dear Single Valentine, we must continue to cling
to the promises of God, and from them never depart.

God has not promised us roses, gifts or candy
filled days, where nothing but good comes our way.
He has promised tribulation and joy unspeakable, but it
is up to us to reach out to Him for comfort, when we pray.

Help us, Lord, not to get caught up in who is dating whom,
and who is on their way down the aisle to "wedded bliss".
Help us, instead, to focus on doing what You have called us to do
for You, so that when our time comes, the Bridegroom we will not miss.

Show us how to keep the oil in our lamps, full and brimming over,
in sacrificial, humble loving ways, as living testaments of self-control.
Dear Lord, strengthen us with patience in the waiting, for in the process,
You are teaching us how to be victoriously single, not fractured, but whole.

February 12, 2004 – Thursday

Michelle Louise Pierre

SINGLE VALENTINE'S HEART

Sitting here at my desk, thinking on the goodness of the Lord, while
cheerfully saying, "Happy Valentine's Day" to all of my young students,
with their eyes beaming so brightly, full of such sweet innocence.
Fully knowing that even though I am still single, this day used to be
one anticipated with a longing and a dread so deep, it could leave
me feeling paralyzed, or in the very least cranky and tense.

But, You, Dear Lord, have come into my heart and forgiven me
for things done foolishly, as I let my lonely heart, time and again,
dictate to me remedies only meant to be temporary, at best.
Dear Lord, thank You, for giving me Your peace that surpasses even
my own understanding; for, surely within human consideration,
I should be feeling hopeless, and more than a little depressed.

Yet, now, I look at the cute, little, red teddy bear given to me by one of
my students this morning, along with a card with a sweet, delicious, red
sucker attached, top-offed with a fourth grader's printing scribbled on it.
To me, this is Your way of telling me, to be grateful for the small things in
life, for out of them, come the blessings that wrap firmly around the soul,
gently, warmly breathing new life into the fertile soil of a humbled spirit.

I am so grateful to You, my sweet Jesus, for You, alone, could mend
this heart, and also give me a new song to sing, as melodies and verses
poetically collide, one after another, right at this moment, in my soul.
Blessed be Your holy and wondrous name, Lord, for taking what was once so
broken by the stinging, bitterness of deception, yet in my repentance, You have
completely restored me, while in submission Your hand, I now firmly can hold.

Therefore, this single valentine's heart, who is so in love and awe of You,
desires above all else to give You, my Lord, praise, glory and honor, for
the divine comfort of the Holy Spirit's tender ministrations, this day.
Heavenly Father, continue to use me for Your glory, as I spend the
rest of this time in the presence of these beautiful children, silently
kneeling my heart in humble adoration, to listen and for them, pray.

February 14, 2006 – Tuesday

In A Solitary Way

SINGLENESS OF HEART

Matthew 5: 13 – 16
Ye are the salt of the earth: but if the salt have lost his savour,
wherewith shall it be salted? it is thenceforth good for nothing,
but to be cast out, and to be trodden under foot of men. Ye are the
light of the world. A city that is set on an hill cannot be hid. Neither do
men light a candle, and put it under a bushel, but on a candlestick;
and it giveth light unto all that are in the house. Let your light
so shine before men, that they may see your good works,
and glorify your Father which is in heaven.

Dear Lord, help me to
answer whenever You call.
Help me to do Your will, even
though I may stumble or fall.

Help me to get back up in
sincere repentance and humility.
Knowing that Your perfecting touch
is constantly at work, reshaping me.

Hold me tightly in the night seasons,
when loneliness claws at my soul.
Speak to me, Lord Jesus, tenderly, persistently
reminding me that heaven must be my goal.

Teach me that contentment must come, whether
I marry, or stay single, for the rest of my life.
I must learn to be willing to lay, even that on the altar,
when compared to Your great merciful sacrifice.

• • •

Strengthen us, anew, in the name of Jesus, that we might
fight this good fight of faith, with true singleness of heart.
Thoroughly bless us, heavenly Father, with the assurance that
Your unconditional love for us, will never lessen or depart.

March 6, 2002 – Wednesday

Michelle Louise Pierre

SINGLY GRACED AND ABUNDANTLY BLESSED

Strutting around the church,
head high in the air.

Knowing that the Lord has your
single soul, in His personal care.

Not paying attention to
those, who simply stare.

You have come to praise the Lord,
that is why you are there.

Hold yourself, daughter, hold yourself, son,
in the manner befitting your call.

This is not a time to come in empty handed,
for you have been chosen to carry the ball.

Hurts, heartaches, traumas and abuses of the past,
no longer show on your face, at all.

Yet, your heart remembers, and you lean even
more fully on the Lord, to never, again, utterly fall.

February 21, 2001 – Wednesday

In A Solitary Way

SO, THIS IS UNCONDITIONAL LOVE?

John 3: 16 – 18
For God so loved the world, that he gave his only begotten Son, that whosoever believeth in him
should not perish, but have everlasting life. For God sent not his Son into the world
to condemn the world; but that the world through him might be saved. He that
believeth on him is not condemned: but he that believeth not is condemned already,
because he hath not believed in the name of the only begotten Son of God.

Feeling rejected and
abandoned, right down
to my very core.
Lord, why in the world
did You permit me fall
to in love with him for?

Daughter, it was to show you
that you could love someone,
over and above your pride.
It was to give you, firsthand
knowledge of how My love
for you has been able to survive.

Father, now that I understand
what it is that You are teaching me,
I am determined to pass this test.
Lord, when I go home tonight,
I will be physically alone, again, help me
to lie down in Your arms, and rest.

I have not spoken to this man,
I chose to set my affections upon,
now, for over forty-eight hours.
Help me to be strong in the waiting,
Lord, because You did not promise us
Growth, without torrential showers.

Lord, I feel that I need You more, now,
than I have ever needed You in this life,
You have so graciously allowed me to see.
Help me to rest, as I give him the space
he requires to work out whatever it is that
is in his heart, keeping him away from me.

I pray in the name of Your Son, Jesus the Christ,
that we, both, remain strong and steadfast
during this time, of forced separation.
May neither of us lose sight of the fact that this
is not about us, but about being even more
productive members of Your holy nation.

Precious Holy Spirit, continue to flow
through our souls giving us what You desire
us to acquire, during this time, as we wait.
Help us to get back together at the appointed
time, if that is Your will, and not allow the enemy
to sow seeds between us, that will make us bait.

Father God, move on our souls as You align our hearts
and minds with the Holy Spirit, who brings comfort,
deliverance, healing and peace from above.
Help us to grow in grace, from glory to glory, for this
time is being used productively to allow us to see,
what is the true meaning of Your unconditional love.

June 7, 2004 – Monday

In A Solitary Way

<u>SOLITUDE</u>

Matthew 6: 5 & 6
And when thou prayest, thou shalt not be as the hypocrites are: for they
love to pray standing in the synagogues and in the corners of the streets,
that they may be seen of men. Verily I say unto you, They have their reward.
But thou, when thou prayest, enter into thy closet, and when thou
hast shut thy door, pray to thy Father which is in secret; and
thy Father which seeth in secret shall reward thee openly.

Matthew 14: 23
And when he had sent the multitudes away,
he went up into a mountain apart to pray: and
when the evening was come, he was there alone.

Blessed, sweet peace
All alone with You

Looking out the window
Rocking slowly in my rocker
Aston-Marie purring at my feet
Mountains in view

Trees almost bare from the winter
Wind blowing amongst the remnant
Leaves, branches blown to and fro

Some leaves freely scatter
No known destination
God is in the wind

Thoughts of Him consume me
He is in my heart

Quiet time, with my Savior
Reflecting upon my life

Repenting for things done in haste
Out of ignorance
Out of a need to belong
Out of a need for human love
Recognition, friendship

Hot tears run down my face, neck
Holy Spirit strokes my brow
I feel so loved

Michelle Louise Pierre

He is the only one
The Holy One
Abba's throne is from everlasting

The world momentarily passes away

Cares systematically flee
As leaves scattered by the wind

They cannot remain

The wind clears my mind

I am forgiven

I am content

I am alone with my God

No pretense

Pure simplicity

He loves me

I love Him

March 23, 1996 – Saturday
(From The Book – Altars Of Praise, Worship, Healing & Deliverance)

In A Solitary Way

STAY OPEN AND STAY HONEST

1 Peter 5: 6 & 7
Humble yourselves therefore under the mighty hand of God,
that he may exalt you in due time: Casting all
your care upon him; for he careth for you.

Dear Lord, God, in Your Son, Jesus', name,
help me to stay open and honest before You.
When I hurt, help me to come straight to You, for
the help, I most assuredly need, in making it through.

Help me to boldly face my fears and not hide them away, so that
others will not see; thereby, being able to be a hindrance, or a help to me.
Help me to humbly bring my soul into submission, with fasting and prayer,
so that I may stand proud and strong before You, not wavering like a new tree.

Never let me, again, seek the cover of darkness to bury
away things, and/or people, whom have caused me pain.
I give You permission, Holy Ghost, to draw me out in the open,
to be nurtured, cleansed and restored by Your healing rain.

• • • • • •

Where else can I go, if not to You, Most Holy High Lord
the lover of my soul and Giver of my blessed life?
For there is no other, who will bear my burdens as You do,
going beyond the realm of father, mother, even husband and wife.

Dear Lord, help me to stay connected to the socket of Your everlasting love that
is being poured out for me, from Your never ending, miraculously healing fountain.
For I know that as I bring my hurts and pains to You, You, alone, are the One,
who will bring me out of the valley, then place me back on the top of Your mountain.

Amen

October 21, 2000 – Saturday
(From The Book – While I Have My Being

Michelle Louise Pierre

STEPPIN' INTO THE NEW!

Psalm 37: 23
The steps of a good man are ordered by the LORD:
and he delighteth in his way.

Jeremiah 1: 4 – 8
Then the word of the LORD came unto me, saying,
Before I formed thee in the belly I knew thee; and before thou camest forth
out of the womb I sanctified thee, and I ordained thee a prophet unto the nations.
Then said I, Ah, Lord GOD! behold, I cannot speak: for I am a child. But the LORD
said unto me, Say not, I am a child: for thou shalt go to all that I shall send thee,
and whatsoever I command thee thou shalt speak. Be not afraid of their faces:
for I am with thee to deliver thee, saith the LORD.

Dear LORD, I am standing on the precipice
of achieving a long standing dream, that along
the way, I did not, at times, fully comprehend
would truly come to fruition or not.
But, by Your grace, I am entering into this
final stage with a rekindled fire, burning deeply
within my soul, that is no longer lukewarm,
but demon rebuking, in the name of Jesus, hot!

This has been a rather long road and I have stumbled
along the way, and even fallen, as my emotions have
led me down paths best left to discussions
with those, who are not faint of heart.
I have repented, forgiven and accepted Your
forgiveness as I have dusted myself off, and
from those carnally induced lustful desires,
once again, withdrew, taking, again, no active part.

• • • • •

I remember when we first met in those early days of college,
as young adult singles, when all of our dreams shone brightly
as the noon day sun; yet, one by one by one, we all seemed
to doggedly rebel against Holy Spirit's inspired intuition.
In the face of all of this, I have also seen friend and foe alike,
succumb to flesh driven needs for love, outside of Your will,
while consequences more dire than we could have ever imagined,
in that stage of our maturity, achingly came to fruition.

In A Solitary Way

Dear LORD, thank You, for saving my soul, restoring
those things broken inside, delivering me, and lovingly healing
me enough to embrace the child of God, whom You created,
before I was formed in my mother's womb, and could come to be.
Father God, You have built within me a love and compassion for
the lost and disenfranchised, that, at times overwhelms my heart;
yet, as feelings of despair and warm tears freely flow, You comfort
my soul by continuously reminding me of my preordained destiny.

. . . . .

Help us, heavenly Father, to never, again, lose sight of
Your grace, as we remain etched in the palm of Your hand,
determined in the power of Your holy might, to remain
humbly submitted, steadfast and faithful, above all, to You.
Help us to successfully proceed, as You have decreed over the
lives of Your children, while preparing to snatch souls from
the fires of hell, covered in the blood of Jesus, eyes forward,
plow in hand, boldly steppin' into uncharted ground, the new.

In Jesus' holy and matchless name, we pray!
Hallelujah and Amen!!!

July 19, 2018 – Thursday

Michelle Louise Pierre

THE BOND OF YOUR LOVE

Strong as a
threefold cord
Knit together
by our LORD

Walking hand in
hand, one day
The Lord teaching
us how to pray

Steeling ourselves
for what lies ahead
Casting out the doubt,
trying to rule our heads

Standing firm on Jesus,
the Savior of our souls
In humble submission,
of all self-willed control

Looking to the Holy Spirit
for comfort and strength
Bowing hearts, together,
as we wholeheartedly repent

Asking the Father to
forgive us of our sins
That done, renewal and
restoration begin to filter in

Stronger now, more secure
in this blessing from above
Thank You, Lord for giving us
the bond of Your love

October 29, 2004 – Friday

In A Solitary Way

THE BOX

Psalm 23: 1 - 4
The LORD is my shepherd; I shall not want.
He maketh me to lie down in green pastures:
he leadeth me beside the still waters.
He restoreth my soul: he leadeth me in the
paths of righteousness for his name's sake.
Yea, though I walk through
the valley of the shadow of death,
I will fear no evil: for thou art with me;
thy rod and thy staff they comfort me.

I can't stay
in the box
I won't, God has
called me out

I can no longer
just sit and stare
God has freed me,
to soar up there

High above my circumstances
and my presumptuous sin
Jesus, sweet Jesus' wounding,
has welcomed me in

• • •

Forgiven and blessed, right down
to the level of marrow and bone
Dear Lord God, no wonder I can
no longer feel, completely, alone

Single in heart, and circumstance,
yet freed to minister freely and to care
Reaching out to wounded hearts, while
showing them how their burdens, You did bare

The Holy Ghost touching the hearts,
of the broken, confused, lost and the lame
Filling them to overflowing, as Your name,
they, too, come to exuberantly proclaim

• • •

Michelle Louise Pierre

Lord, thank You for poking holes in my box,
so that the light of Your love could stream in
Thank You, precious, wonderful Jesus,
for being my Savior and Friend

Now, the world can no longer claim me as a victim,
caught in its whirling, destructive paradox
My Heavenly Father, has set me free,
I will not be put back in that box

July 17, 1999 – Thursday
(From The Book – A Pen Of Iron)

In A Solitary Way

THE CRUSH OF LONELINESS

Ephesians 6: 10 – 18
Finally, my brethren, be strong in the Lord, and in the power of his might.
Put on the whole armour of God, that ye may be able to stand against the wiles of the devil.
For we wrestle not against flesh and blood, but against principalities, against powers,
against the rulers of the darkness of this world, against spiritual wickedness in high places.
Wherefore take unto you the whole armour of God, that ye may be able to withstand
in the evil day, and having done all, to stand. Stand therefore, having your loins girt
about with truth, and having on the breastplate of righteousness; And your feet shod
with the preparation of the gospel of peace; Above all, taking the shield of faith,
wherewith ye shall be able to quench all the fiery darts of the wicked. And take
the helmet of salvation, and the sword of the Spirit, which is the word of God

Walked into a room filled with people, laughing and talking,
who had found their seats earlier; as you walk up to them,
you notice they have extended no effort to make room for you.
In fact, you realize it is not even a thought in their consciousness,
for they have been "paired" up so long, they may have forgotten, or may
simply never have known, what some single Christians, at times, go through.

However, the enemy was there, with deception, quick as a lick, to reintroduce
you to the spirit of rejection with its fetid breath, waiting along with the companion
spirit of abandonment, both jockeying for position, trying to gain a solid foothold.
You stand there, as it hits you like a ton of bricks, yet determined to shake it off, you
turn to find a seat; at the same time, bringing out your cell phone to pass the time, waiting
for the beginning of praise and worship, to fill the atmosphere as God's love takes hold.

During praise and worship, as you sing out from the depths of your soul, while the
crush of loneliness, again, tries to get you to step out from under the protective covering you
have mercifully found, only in trusting the LORD, tucked safely under the shadow of His wings.
The music plays as you continue to press into the praise, tambourine now in hand, while beginning to
feel a shifting on the inside that permeates your soul, taking you higher in the Spirit, touching God's
heart, shattering the grip of the enemy's tricks, you respond by giving Jesus your all, your everything!

March 28, 2018 – Wednesday

Michelle Louise Pierre

THE DOOR OF YOUR HEART

Matthew 13: 24 - 30
Another parable put he forth unto them, saying, The kingdom of heaven is likened unto a man which sowed good seed in his field: But while men slept, his enemy came and sowed tares among the wheat, and went his way. But when the blade was sprung up, and brought forth fruit, then appeared the tares also. So the servants of the householder came and said unto him, Sir, didst not thou sow good seed in thy field? from whence then hath it tares? He said unto them, An enemy hath done this. The servants said unto him, Wilt thou then that we go and gather them up? But he said, Nay; lest while ye gather up the tares, ye root up also the wheat with them. Let both grow together until the harvest: and in the time of harvest I will say to the reapers, Gather ye together first the tares, and bind them in bundles to burn them: but gather the wheat into my barn.

There is a new man on
the horizon, and at this point,
I don't know if he will come
In for a landing, or fly right by.
I am leaving this new relationship
firmly in Your hands, for Your still,
small voice is my spiritual command
center, prompting me from on High.

Be in the midst, oh LORD,
because we, Your children desire
not to veer, ever again, off of
Your predestined course.
Develop this relationship,
naturally, let it flow as a river,
bringing life, not death, with
healthy free will, not force.

Continue to build in our hearts an
unquenchable desire to know You
in ways more intimate than either
of us have ever experienced before.
For, only in that place of divine intimacy
will we unerringly be able to hear You say,
clearly to our singly beating hearts, and minds,
"Now, you can open, or close, that door."

February 16, 2006 – Thursday

In A Solitary Way

THE GATE

Matthew 14: 26 – 31
And when the disciples saw him walking on the sea, they were troubled, saying,
It is a spirit; and they cried out for fear. But straightway Jesus spake unto them, saying,
Be of good cheer; it is I; be not afraid. And Peter answered him and said, Lord, if it
be thou, bid me come unto thee on the water. And he said, Come. And when Peter
was come down out of the ship, he walked on the water, to go to Jesus. But when
he saw the wind boisterous, he was afraid; and beginning to sink, he cried, saying,
Lord, save me. And immediately Jesus stretched forth his hand, and caught him,
and said unto him, O thou of little faith, wherefore didst thou doubt?

John 14: 25 – 27
These things have I spoken unto you, being yet present with you. But the Comforter,
which is the Holy Ghost, whom the Father will send in my name, he shall teach you all things,
and bring all things to your remembrance, whatsoever I have said unto you. Peace I leave
with you, my peace I give unto you: not as the world giveth, give I unto you.
Let not your heart be troubled, neither let it be afraid.

It is time, My daughter
Father, I am too afraid
I will be with you, My child
Total healing lies just beyond these doors
It is time to enter in

In the past
Liberty glimpsed, not able to hold
True love, before unknown, slipping your grasp
Shackles just broken, not destroyed

Now
Hope renewed, given wings of the morning sun
Brightly, brightly shining sweetly on the needy soul
Freedom, My daughter, freedom

The time has come for you to see, in its entirety
I am ready, Father, hold me close
I am with you, darling, don't let go
One step at a time
The pace has been unequivocally slow

Slowed down to prepare you
Resting your soul, between steps
Joy at each level, savored
Not knowing what was in store

Michelle Louise Pierre

Casting your cares truly upon Me
At times, a major chore
Learning to love Me
Learning to accept My love, in its purest form

No strings, no fine print
Learning to love yourself
Struggling to love those, who have hurt you
Learning, at last, to love them, too
Learning the ultimate meaning of love

Divinely inspired, flowing lovingly from My breast
Nourished by My love alone
This has been the task set before you
This deliverance has taken five years
With Me lovingly leading the way
You, at times, stumbling but getting right back up

Now, daughter, there is one last hurdle left to take
One that will set your soul totally free from its past

Do not hesitate, even though pain is not a place
Where you willingly choose to visit

This is for your own good
You must trust Me, My child
Cling even more tightly to Me

Come into My arms, daughter
Recline into My bosom
I will bring you beyond the seal
Beyond the veil, now dropping from your eyes

As we go, trample
Annihilate
All of the snakes of

Rejection, heartache
Loneliness, self-hatred
Abandonment, molestation
Physical abuse, emotional abuse

I have given you the power to destroy them all
They hiss, slithering in front of the door
Daring you to try to come further in

You have come too far
No turning back, this time
The strength needed is not yours
It is Mine

In A Solitary Way

Do not try to skirt around them
They can hurt you, no longer
I have taken away their deceptive, poisonous sting
Each bold step crushes another one under your feet

Leave them as chaff in the wind of My nostrils
I created you strong
Be that for Me
Be that for yourself
Be that, for the others
Whom you will be used to set free

Let My love for you
strengthen each step
Now, look back
See My deliverance of your soul

You survived, My daughter
You survived

My loving rest and abundant life awaits
Prepare to meet the you, I created you to be

Hand on the door

Turn the knob

Now, enter in by the gate

December 26, 1997 – Friday
(From The Book – Speaking In The Light)

Michelle Louise Pierre

THE HEALING SEASON

John 5: 1 - 4
After this there was a feast of the Jews; and Jesus went up to Jerusalem. Now there is at Jerusalem by the sheep market a pool, which is called in the Hebrew tongue Bethesda, having five porches. In these lay a great multitude of impotent folk, of blind, halt, withered, waiting for the moving of the water. For an angel went down at a certain season into the pool, and troubled the water: whosoever then first after the troubling of the water stepped in was made whole of whatsoever disease he had.

Lord, prepare me to be a sanctuary, pure and holy,
where Your healing virtues may pour through me.
Bring healing to my innermost parts; then,
flow out to all of mankind, which is my destiny.

Heal hearts, minds, bodies and souls, prompting us,
Your children, to labor on our own, as well as other's behalf.
Fortify us, daily, with Your pervasive, healing ministrations,
leading us through valleys green, with Your rod and staff.

As You lead us through places where wise men
fear to tread, fortify our hearts with Your strength.
Teach us to fear no evil, as You prompt our hearts to
extend the rope of hope, without thought of the length.

Birth in us a fire that is unquenchable by the enemy's darts,
because it was stoked at the hearth of Your loving sacrifice.
For, if You had not chosen to die for our sins, we would not be
in existence, much less be able to even draw breath, in this life.

May we be bold in our pursuit of You, by allowing no one or thing,
to persuade us from our course, with worldly lures or manmade reason.
Most of all Dear Lord, may we bravely cast our cares upon You, receiving
Your care, in return, as we walk away whole, during this, our healing season.

March 6, 2001 – Tuesday

In A Solitary Way

THE LAND OF REGRET

2 Timothy 3: 1 – 7
This know also, that in the last days perilous times shall come. For men shall be lovers of their own selves, covetous, boasters, proud, blasphemers, disobedient to parents, unthankful, unholy, Without natural affection, trucebreakers, false accusers, incontinent, fierce, despisers of those that are good, Traitors, heady, highminded, lovers of pleasures more than lovers of God; Having a form of godliness, but denying the power thereof: from such turn away. For of this sort are they which creep into houses, and lead captive silly women laden with sins, led away with divers lusts, Ever learning, and never able to come to the knowledge of the truth.

Dear Lord, help me, I don't want to wake up,
one day, in the wretched "Land of Regret".
Arrived at, like so many other women I know, by
compromising Godly values, for a man they just met.

As for me, he really does seem nice, but is
asking for something that I am not willing to give.
I made a vow to You, Lord, years ago,
and it is a celibate, chaste life I now live.

He says he does not want sex, just that when
he visits, we sleep under the same roof.
I made that vow, this time, to remain pure before
marriage, in that I intend to stand, without reproof.

I explained all this to this Christian man, and
his response was that I was being dogmatic.
Then he cleanly dropped the subject, because
pursuing it, would only lead to further static.

If he is out of my life, then obviously, he was simply
in the way of the right one, I have not yet met.
For Lord, with all of my heart, as I counsel these women,
Help me not to end up, myself, in the "Land of Regret".

October 11, 2003 – Saturday

Michelle Louise Pierre

THE MEASURE OF FAITH

Romans 12: 3
For I say, through the grace given unto me, to every man that is among you,
not to think of himself more highly than he ought to think; but to think soberly,
according as God hath dealt to every man the measure of faith.

Strengthen us, in our season of singleness, oh Lord, as we step
into a realm where faith must take precedence over fleshly desires.
Let us not be led astray, by the complacency of worldly allure,
as it comes to quench this God ordained baptism by spiritual fire!

Dear Lord, forgive us for the times when fear rose up
to a level, where faith was forced to take a back seat.
For surely, these are the times that try the hearts of man;
help us to stand in the face off all fear, and not retreat!

Teach us to plead the blood of Jesus over every situation in
our lives, as we allow the Holy Spirit to be our daily guide.
Cast down those things within us, that oppose Your blessed
holy will, from taking the reins on this heavenward ride!

Increase the measure of faith that we need to storm the gates of hell,
taking captive those bound for destruction, regardless of how we may feel.
Dear High, Holy LORD, burn off the dross in our hearts, lighting the fire
brightly, not lukewarm, for our love of You must be unquenchable and real!

2 Corinthians 10: 4 – 5
For the weapons of our warfare are not carnal, but mighty through God
to the pulling down of strong holds; Casting down imaginations, and
every high thing that exalteth itself against the knowledge of God, and
bringing into captivity every thought to the obedience of Christ.

In Jesus' holy name and for His sake, we pray.
Hallelujah and Amen!!!

September 26, 2004 – Sunday

In A Solitary Way

THE OFFERING

Psalm 51: 12 – 17
Restore unto me the joy of thy salvation; and uphold me with thy free spirit.
Then will I teach transgressors thy ways; and sinners shall be converted unto thee.
Deliver me from bloodguiltiness, O God, thou God of my salvation: and my tongue
shall sing aloud of thy righteousness. O Lord, open thou my lips; and my mouth shall
shew forth thy praise. For thou desirest not sacrifice; else would I give it: thou
delightest not in burnt offering. The sacrifices of God are a broken spirit:
a broken and a contrite heart, O God, thou wilt not despise.

Where is your offering?

Father said
Untainted, unblemished sacrifice
Not second-rate castaways
He wants only the best for you
Why give Him, anything less?
If it does not cost you something
Keep it for yourself

• • •

You come to realize
Things take longer than you expect
Perfecting the gift, to offer
Unto the living God

He will accept no dead praise
Praise must live
Abundance of life, worship
Life lived with joy, contentment
Certifiably true, missionary zeal

Spiritual revolt
This happiness is new to your soul
Wants sadness, depression back
Seeks opportunities to suck you back in
Finds an open door

Discernment takes hold
Repentance closes the door by the blood of Jesus
The Holy Spirit rises to your defense
Angels protect with swords of fire
The gates of your heart

Michelle Louise Pierre

The veil finally, permanently lifts
His wondrous light shines through
You see Him on His divine throne

In His marvelous Kingdom
"Holy, Holy, Holy", fills the atmosphere

Doubts, fears flee
Searching for obscurity
Can't stand the purity of the light
Bundled up, bound securely, freely given
Holding nothing back, revealing all in humility

You place yourself back in His hands
Vowing never to leave, again

He washes your soul

Whiter than snow

He has accepted

Your offering

February 29, 1996 – Thursday
(From The Book – Altars of Praise, Worship, Healing & Deliverance)

In A Solitary Way

THE ONION

John 15: 1 - 5
I am the true vine, and my Father is the husbandman. Every branch in me
that beareth not fruit he taketh away: and every branch that beareth fruit,
he purgeth it, that it may bring forth more fruit. Now ye are clean through
the word which I have spoken unto you. Abide in me, and I in you.
As the branch cannot bear fruit of itself, except it abide in the vine;
no more can ye, except ye abide in me. I am the vine, ye are the
branches: He that abideth in me, and I in him, the same
bringeth forth much fruit: for without me ye can do nothing.

Preparations for a feast
Sharpened blade, held firmly in skilled hands
All of the ingredients lined up on the counter
Ready to chop, peel, slice, dice
Drop in the simmering pot
One last thing to do
Peel the onion

The first few layers are easy
They are weak, paper thin, flimsy, fragile
They fall away quickly
The next layer, closest to the actual meat
Requires slightly more effort
After all, they contain thin layers of the flesh
Cutting into them, eases the removal process
Now the real fun begins
You are now ready to slice it completely open

Once cut, nose starts to twitch
Now eyes seem on perpetual fire
Flowing, uncontrollable tears
Do not bring comfort
Do not soothe the stinging eyes
Cut out the core, slice into the meat
Can hardly see, because of the burning
The tears pouring out and down
The job still remains to be done

You proceed full steam ahead
Realization, your vision is being impaired
You slow down the knife
Splash water in your eyes
Clears your vision
Take inventory of your fingers
Make a visual check, of their imminent location

Michelle Louise Pierre

Secure, much more slowly, this time
Completing the project with your own safety
Now, foremost in your mind

You throw the useless parts away
You add the useful parts to the pot

. . . . .

View your life as an onion
Jesus is Lord, but...

Unhappy, discontented
Ill at ease within yourself
Compulsive, short tempered
Judgmental, painfully shy
Withdrawn, mean-spirited
Obsessive, self-conscious
Irrational jealousies, flood your mind

No faith, no hope
Inability to trust anyone
Ready to give up
Fear of intimacy and love
No matter whose hand offers it
Bondage

Layers and layers
Surround your soul
When brought to the light
Will sting, will burn,
Will bring tears to your eyes

You want to cut right to the core of your pain
Christ stays your hand
You are not ready
To see what is under the next layer
Before its predetermined time

Too soon, would destroy your soul
Too late, would cause rottenness, bitterness

You cannot handle it, yet
He slows you down, again

He helps you take a mental, spiritual inventory
He splashes water in your eyes
By means of the Holy Ghost
Clears your vision
This brings you true, lasting comfort

In A Solitary Way

He gently nudges you to continue on
You find that you no longer feel alone
You have finally allowed Him
The opportunity to love you

His love brings healing strength
He becomes your eyes
Your teacher

He leads you on
Step by step, gentle persistence
For each sting of revelation
He is your salve, your balm
Deeper and deeper, you cut within

All is now revealed
This is a process
Days, months, years have gone by
You are, now, strong

• • • • •

The onion is now ready to join the feast
The useless parts are thrown away
The useful parts are saved
Added to the pot of a productive
Fulfilling, godly life

As an onion carefully peeled
Cut, sliced, chopped, diced
You have been laid open
Washed clean, purified

Now
Meat for the Master's use

July 23, 1996 - Tuesday
(From The Book – Speaking In The Light)

Michelle Louise Pierre

THE VOICE OF MY BELOVED

Song of Solomon 5:2
I sleep, but my heart waketh:
it is the voice of my beloved that knocketh,
saying, Open to me, my sister, my love, my dove,
my undefiled: for my head is filled with dew,
and my locks with the drops of the night.

Dear LORD, I hear the voice of my Beloved,
From a distance, calling sweetly, soothingly, unto me.
It is a call once extremely faint, now heard loudly,
speaking boldly of our combined destiny.

It is saying that I can trust him, as he will
do me good and not harm, all the days of our life.
You are telling us that we were created to be joined in
holy matrimony, one glorious day, as husband and wife.

Then we will run into each other's arms, seeking
only the comforting love found encircled within.
Staying there forever, Dear LORD, as You prune dead,
useless things from our lives, stirring up repentance from sin.

Precious Holy Spirit, thank You, for all the times You brought
conviction, without compromise, prompting us to go the narrow way.
LORD, thank You for making us one with Your Spirit, for in submission,
may we honor You, by living for Your glory, each and every day.

In Jesus' name, we make our requests
known to You, as we pray.
Thank You and Amen!

July 18, 2006 – Tuesday

TOO BLESSED TO BE DEPRESSED!

Psalm 5: 11 & 12
But let all those that put their trust in thee rejoice:
let them ever shout for joy, because thou defendest them:
let them also that love thy name be joyful in thee. For thou,
LORD, wilt bless the righteous; with favour wilt
thou compass him as with a shield.

Hallelujah! Blessed be the name of the Lord!
My heart is pumping in pure joy, on one heavenly accord.

The Lord is my King, my Savior and my beloved Friend.
This joy has captured my spirit, sanctifying it from deeply within.

Hallelujah! Blessed beyond measure, beyond all hope.
Feet given the wings of the morning, no stress of which, together, we cannot cope.

Abba has bathed me in His love and adored me, since before time could begin.
Whirling around this room, shouting out my love for Him, signifying the state that I am in.

Hallelujah! Blessed to the very depths of a once battered, lonely soul.
Body, now, realigned to offer up praises to my Lord, far beyond human control.

To the world, my heart should be heavy, Christmas is coming, without children or mate.
Glory be to God for His love is massaging the cockles of my being, this very date.

Hallelujah! Blessed to the point of feeling His arms surrounding me like a sleeping bag.
Tingling at His touch, as I skip along in the Spirit, like a child joyfully playing tag.

It is not that I do not desire to have children or a mate one of these days, for I do.
Casting out doubt, instead choosing, to praise God for all that He has brought me through.

Hallelujah! Blessed and relaxing, all curled up in the hem of Jehovah-Jireh's garment.
Not letting the enemy win this battle for possession of my soul, to lead me to torment.

It is more than a cute saying on a bumper sticker, designed by someone to alleviate stress.
I am loved beyond measure by the Holy Trinity, I am too blessed to be depressed!

December 23, 1999 – Thursday
(From The Book – While I Have My Being)

Michelle Louise Pierre

UNFULFILLED LIFE

Ecclesiastes 3: 1 – 7
To every thing there is a season,
and a time to every purpose under the heaven:
A time to be born, and a time to die;
a time to plant, and a time to pluck up that which is planted;
A time to kill, and a time to heal; a time to break down, and a time to build up;
A time to weep, and a time to laugh; a time to mourn, and a time to dance;
A time to cast away stones, and a time to gather stones together;
a time to embrace, and a time to refrain from embracing;
A time to get, and a time to lose;
a time to keep, and a time to cast away;
A time to rend, and a time to sew;
a time to keep silence, and a time to speak

Dear Christian Friend,
God has shown you some wonderful things
Things He has said that you can achieve
Confirmation has come on all sides
His holy Word speaks to your heart

Other people have come up to you to share a word
Even the pastor touched upon your special area of ministry
But, you are too busy to stop and turn around
Too busy, to pursue God's vision with a vengeance
Too many things are going wrong in your life

Your rent is due today
You won't have the money, until next week
You hope that the check
The one you wrote for groceries, is not going to bounce
Your children are totally out of control

You feel like you are losing your mind
Almost wishing that you were, as a form of escape
With all that is going on in your life
With all of the decisions that you have to make

You cannot afford to take the time, to study God's Word
You simply have too much to do
Too many balls to keep up in the air

Now, this guy has been calling you from work
He doesn't want any type of commitment
Just got out of a long-term relationship
Simply wants you as a friend
That's what he says

In A Solitary Way

But, his actions speak differently
He is full of romantic innuendoes and gestures
To get inside your door, after midnight
Alluding to "should have beens"
"Would have beens"
"Wish it could have been"
As he continues to skirt around the real issue
Putting his pants back on, one leg at a time
Leaving you feeling used, and empty inside

Now, you want more from the relationship
He wants to keep it the same
Not knowing your own worth
Your value in God's eyes

Like a little abandoned, stray dog or cat
You settle for the scraps
He chooses to throw your way

This has been going on for years
Friends have tired of hearing about this one-sided situation
He still longs for his past relationship
They can see it clearly, you cannot
Still, hope springs eternal
You decide to "hang in there"

The other problems still exist
Church going, also now requires too much time
You have decided to take on another job
Surely, God is in the midst of all your decisions

Some of the balls are finally balanced
Making a perfect arc, as you juggle on
Others simply dropped, been forgotten about
After all, there is always tomorrow

Your children will mature, on their own, eventually
Thereby, completely getting out of your hair
Until then, let God direct their steps

No time to cook anymore
You plan your meals around
Take-out menus and fast food joints

You know better
The doctor has warned you
Not once, several times

Hey, no time to exercise either
Your health is deteriorating

Michelle Louise Pierre

Bad nutrition is taking its toll
The stress of making wrong choices
Wearing you down to a frazzle

Then, your body goes into shock
Heart attack, they say
You, simply stunned, dazed
All those other things
Don't seem so important anymore

Light can finally penetrate the darkness
You have built around your soul
You decide it's time to pray

Regrets rise to the surface
Like oil separating from water

You are now flat on your back, immobilized
Plenty of time to review your life's choices
Scenes flash, moods captured in time
You ask yourself, what have you done with your life?

Opportunities to grow closer to the Lord
Pushed foolishly aside, time and time, again
Chasing fantasies of your own making
Not seeking the direction
That only the Holy Spirit can provide

Hot, bitter tears of repentance
Run down the creases in your tired, weary face
Pleas for forgiveness bombard your fearful mind
You are crying out to the Father for mercy
Begging for another chance to get it right

This time, you promise
You won't put Him in last place
Peace like a river washes over your soul
You feel His loving, forgiving touch

Smiling in the midst of the storm
Remembering all of the times of sweet fellowship
You and He used to share
Catching your breath, feeling your heart relax
You make plans for your future

This time you will keep your commitments
You vow, you will be a better parent
You will be a wise steward of God's money
You will break free of that dead relationship
Etcetera, etcetera, etcetera

In A Solitary Way

Friends and family come by to offer comfort
Drawing heavily upon their own measure of faith
Allaying their own fears, putting on a "happy face"
You, in turn, share your hopes and dreams

Your room turns into a prayer meeting
With every visitor, gladly taking a turn
There is truly strength in numbers
You feel a surge in your spirit

Alone again
Another visiting hour, over for the day
Hooked up to all types of monitors
Observing the beating of your own heart

Each new peak and valley
Slicing through the darkened screen
Adding light, visibly demonstrating hope
Each beep sounding strong and sure
Strengthening your resolve

Given the time, you will make amends
Seeing all of the opportunities, that you have missed
All of the wrong turns that have led you amiss
You know you have been given a second chance

You take the time to thank God profusely
Your love for Him, overwhelming and sure
Now stronger than ever before

Peace enters the room

You see the eternal light

A warmth encases your soul

The blip on the screen goes flat

October 9, 1996 – Wednesday
(From The Book – Speaking In The Light)

Michelle Louise Pierre

WHAT DO PEOPLE SEE?

1 Samuel 16: 7
But the LORD said unto Samuel,
Look not on his countenance,
or on the height of his stature;
because I have refused him:
for the LORD seeth not as man seeth;
for man looketh on the outward appearance,
but the LORD looketh on the heart.

What do people see, when they, really, look at you?

Do they see the pain that you still harbor inside?
Do they see the shyness, formulated from years of rejection?
Do they see the smile, that doesn't quite reach the eyes?
Do they hear the heart pounding with fear within your chest?
Do they see the hint of a wounded child cringing within?
Do they see the little boy, too afraid to be a man?
Do they see the man hiding behind the little boy facade?
Do they see the little girl desperately needing love?
Do they see the woman hiding behind the little girl facade?
Do they see hollow eyes, filled with the darkness of the past,
with a routine "Praise God" flowing from your lips?
Do they see the child beaten down so badly, so constantly,
as to remain permanently bent over in the spirit and the flesh?
Do they see that your moods change quicker than the weather?
Do they see that you are more concerned with pleasing man, than God?
Do they see you using guilt, like a spoiled child uses a pout, to get your way?
Do they see the hatred, kindled by a perpetual fire burning inside?
Do they see the prejudices ingrained by parents, who knew only pain?
Do they see the malignancy of the spiritual cancer, eating away at your joy?
Do they see the false pride, vying for center stage, fueled by feeling of inferiority?
Do they see the shallowness of your root system, choking to death for need of truth?
Do they see the secrets, lies and other hidden things that lie buried deep within?
Do they see the child, whose only comfort was the warmth of the tears upon their face?
Do they see the fear of exposure, that causes you to run from any new friend?
Do they see self-pity so strongly entrenched in your spirit that they want to flee?
Do they see you "get busy" in the church, to hide your lack of fellowship with the Lord?

Or ...

Do they see the child that no one loved, but Jesus?
Do they see Jesus, in you, so as to cover a multitude of sins?
Do they see the Holy Spirit's comforting ministrations making you whole?
Do they see that you are a living epistle, being written by the hand of the Father?
Do they see you ministering through to the other side of your hurt and your fears?
Do they see you drinking from the fountain of living water that will never run dry?
Do they see you learning the lessons that the Lord came to teach?

In A Solitary Way

Do they see you loving, when all that is within you wants to hate?
Do they see you giving, when all that you really want to do is take?

Do they see you isolated for trying to live a life of holiness, a cut above the rest?
Do they see you knocked down, but calling out to Jesus for help?
Do they see you rising above your circumstances, giving all glory to the Lord?
Do they see you working towards becoming the man, God created you to be?
Do they see you working towards becoming the woman, God birthed within?
Do they see the love of Jesus, in all that you do or say?
Do they see that salvation is firmly nestled in your countenance?
Do they see that you would give your life for the Lord?
Do they see that you are a person of honest integrity?
Do they see you humbly submit to the Lord for correction and guidance when needed?
Do they see that you have no fear of the enemy, because of the God that you serve?
Do they see that you are not afraid to be made vulnerable,
as you put all of your trust in the finished work of Calvary?
Do they see repentance flood your soul, immediately after doing wrong?
Do they see that the ability to forgive and ask for forgiveness is dear to your soul?
Do they see your eyes light up when you speak of the goodness of the Lord?
Do they see that you are determined to worship and praise Him, above all?
Do they see the tenderness of your soul as it is laid bare before them?
Do they see the Father sitting at the potter's wheel of your heart?

. . . . .

What exactly do people see, when they look at you?

Psalm 51: 1 – 4, 10 – 14
Have mercy upon me, O God, according to thy lovingkindness:
according unto the multitude of thy tender mercies blot out my transgressions.
Wash me throughly from mine iniquity, and cleanse me from my sin.
For I acknowledge my transgressions: and my sin is ever before me.
Against thee, thee only, have I sinned, and done this evil in thy sight:
that thou mightest be justified when thou speakest, and be clear when thou judgest.
…Create in me a clean heart, O God; and renew a right spirit within me.
Cast me not away from thy presence; and take not thy holy spirit from me.
Restore unto me the joy of thy salvation; and uphold me with thy free spirit.
Then will I teach transgressors thy ways; and sinners shall be converted unto thee.
Deliver me from bloodguiltiness, O God, thou God of my salvation:
and my tongue shall sing aloud of thy righteousness.

March 2, 1998 – Monday
(From The Book – Speaking In The Light)

Michelle Louise Pierre

WHEN AN INTERCESSOR WEEPS

1 Samuel 30: 3, 4, 6, 8 & 19
So David and his men came to the city, and, behold, it was burned with fire; and their wives, and their sons, and their daughters, were taken captives. Then David and the people that were with him lifted up their voice and wept, until they had no more power to weep. ...And David was greatly distressed; for the people spake of stoning him, because the soul of all the people was grieved, every man for his sons and for his daughters: but David encouraged himself in the LORD his God. ...And David inquired at the LORD, saying, Shall I pursue after this troop? shall I overtake them? And he answered him, Pursue: for thou shalt surely overtake them, and without fail recover all. ...And there was nothing lacking to them, neither small nor great, neither sons nor daughters, neither spoil, nor any thing that they had taken to them: David recovered all.

Pray, Dear Intercessor, and let the Lord use you to purge and pour
healing love out to the nations, to the people, who stand in need.
Pray, in submission and humility for His Kingdom to truly come and
His will to be done on this earth, as hungry souls those prayers feed.

Pray as hot tears stream down your face, because you are touching the
heart of God, feeling His love extending to those who cannot, will not, pray.
Pray as He moves through your soul, using you as a conduit to bring restoration
and holy comfort, on a level that is way beyond the mere words you say.

Pray in the Spirit, as the Lord leads you down the paths He desires,
regardless of your personal feelings about how badly someone has behaved.
Pray for the Holy Ghost to have free reign in their lives, and for Jesus Christ,
to be invited into the hearts, He bled and died, on that cross to save.

Pray for those, who have used and abused you, too, for in so doing you are releasing
yourself into the atmosphere of healing forgiveness, from the prison of bitter hate.
Pray, also, when the Lord brings a face or name before you, without taking the time
to wonder what their need is, for the Father certainly knows and He is just that great!

Pray for yourself to be covered in the blood of Jesus' protective healing love, as He
stills the beating of your heart, placing you back in bed, lovingly rocking you to sleep.
Knowing that the Lord is interceding on your behalf, and those whom you have obediently
lifted up to Him, as you, have allowed Him through your intercessor's heart to weep.

September 24, 2002 - Tuesday
(From The Book – A Consuming Fire)

In A Solitary Way

WHEN FAITH MEETS THE FIRE!

Daniel 3: 22 – 25
Therefore because the king's commandment was urgent, and the furnace exceeding hot,
the flame of the fire slew those men that took up Shadrach, Meshach, and Abednego.
And these three men, Shadrach, Meshach, and Abednego, fell down bound into the midst
of the burning fiery furnace. Then Nebuchadnezzar the king was astonied, and rose up in haste,
and spake, and said unto his counsellors, Did not we cast three men bound into the midst of the fire?
They answered and said unto the king, True, O king. He answered and said, Lo, I see four men loose,
walking in the midst of the fire, and they have no hurt; and the form of the fourth is like the Son of God.

1 Peter 1: 7 – 9
That the trial of your faith, being much more precious than of gold that perisheth, though it be
tried with fire, might be found unto praise and honour and glory at the appearing of Jesus Christ:
Whom having not seen, ye love; in whom, though now ye see him not, yet believing, ye rejoice with
joy unspeakable and full of glory: Receiving the end of your faith, even the salvation of your souls.

When faith meets the fire,
My Daughter, how will you dance?
Will you go back to the world,
to assume an ungodly stance?

Will you yet stand on the victory in
My Son, Jesus, on which you teach?
Will you humble your heart,
allowing Me to speak and do in-reach?

Will the Holy Spirit truly be
allowed to comfort your heart?
Will you lean more fully on Me,
accepting the call on you, to be set apart?

Will you remember that I am with you
always, even until the end of the world?
Will you crawl into my arms, for
I know you are but dust, My baby girl?

Even now, I am sending the holy comfort you need
in this time that, for most, would be so dire.
But, I know through all these years of service to Me,
you have the sustaining faith that will meet the fire!

April 2, 2018 – Monday
(Taken From – As For Me And My House)

Michelle Louise Pierre

WHEN I MET JESUS, FOR THE FIRST TIME

Revelation 12: 11
And they overcame him by the blood of the Lamb,
and by the word of their testimony;
and they loved not their lives unto the death.

My name is Michelle Louise Pierre, and I have
been divorced since December of 1985,
as some of you may already know.
I am now putting the finishing touches on
a book for singles, as the LORD nudges me
back to that time, that now seems so long ago.

Still, I can remember that time, like looking back
at the photos in an old album; but, instead of joy,
I can recall it left me, at times, just struck dumb.
In fact, if the LORD was not prompting me to put
these words down, I would gladly leave them out; for
there were times when I wept so deeply, it left me numb.

Yet, more often than not, I went about my daily tasks,
as I always have, while I stoically put on
a brave face, for the world outside.
I did my laundry, I washed my car, I visited relatives;
yet, all the while the only thing that I really wanted
to do was close the door, be alone, and stay inside.

So much has gone on in my life since then, but I feel
the LORD is urging me to take the time, before closing this
book forever, to write this portion of my testimony down.
I know, as I knew it then, that without a shadow of a doubt,
my sanity and sobriety were at stake, if I had not allowed
Jesus Christ to come in, and my soul, surround.

For you see, unbeknownst to all the people in my life,
whenever I was by myself, in order to numb the pain,
I would drink alcohol and weep, all weekend long.
Then, as I had learned to do from childhood, not
to show my true emotions, I would get myself up,
get ready for work, and act like nothing was wrong.

This went on for three months, and it was on
one of these benders, that I rolled off my bed,
and found myself flat out on the floor.
In my drunken, weepy state, a moment of clarity came in,
as I thought of my alcoholic father, and I realized that
was the road I, too, was headed down, for sure.

On that day, July 7, 1984, I cried out to the LORD, as never before;
for to me, He was someone whom, although raised before the age
of eighteen in a Lutheran church, I had never really personally known.
I reached for a tattered piece of paper, and wrote, "Help me, Jesus!"
in red ink, the only color pen I could find at the time; even now, I can
remember that all around me, still on the floor, a bright light was shown.

I will never, ever be able to fully express my gratefulness to the LORD, for His
unfailing love and patience with me, time and time, again, as I have vacillated
between being real and sold out, and, at other times, being a hypocritical phony.
Now, I find that I have to choose to be real with what is going on in my own heart;
for, in exposing it to the light, I hope to share this victory with others, about God's
unconditional love and amazing grace, with this, one brief portion of my testimony.

Revelation 12: 10 & 11
And I heard a loud voice saying in heaven,
Now is come salvation, and strength, and the kingdom of our God, and the power of his Christ:
for the accuser of our brethren is cast down, which accused them before our God day and night.
And they overcame him by the blood of the Lamb, and by the word of their testimony;
and they loved not their lives unto the death.

October 27, 2006 – Friday

Michelle Louise Pierre

WHO IS ON THE LORD'S SIDE?

Exodus 32: 26
Then Moses stood in the gate of the camp, and said,
Who is on the LORD'S side? let him come unto me.
And all the sons of Levi gathered themselves together unto him.

Joshua 24: 15
And if it seem evil unto you to serve the LORD, choose you this day whom
ye will serve; whether the gods which your fathers served that were on the other
side of the flood, or the gods of the Amorites, in whose land ye dwell:
but as for me and my house, we will serve the LORD.

Wake up, stand up, and fight in
the power of God's holy might!
For the enemy is battling for your soul,
my friend, this very moment, this night!

This enemy, God's enemy, has decided
that he has created the perfect bait.
You have been battling lust, and have
tired of waiting for your godly mate.

This snare is being set so your soul, will end
up in the enemy's hellish place of unrest.
Get on your knees, right now, humble your
heart before God, I pray you pass this test.

Don't give in, even if he did come with supposedly
a real diamond ring that can be seen "six blocks away".
For to let your heart be seduced by delusions of worldly
wealth untold, will cause your soul's utter decay.

The Lord created you to be a precious, flawless
jewel in His crown, not a ring in a pig's snout.
Come to yourself, as did the prodigal son,
before it is too late to seek God's narrow way out.

For in the confusion of the tricks with lights and mirrors, flashed in
your gullible eyes, dear single mother, you have begun to stumble.
Spiraling down one inch at a time, so subtly that this trip down,
from which I pray when you awake, will leave you irrevocably humble.

Further, I pray that when you do "come to yourself", you will remember
that there is no condemnation for those, who belong to the Lord.
My prayer is that you, and your children, will come to the other side of this,
more strongly enfolded and permanently entwined with the Lord, on one accord.

In A Solitary Way

• • • • •

Dear Heavenly Father God,

Cover them in the blood of Your holy Son, Jesus the Christ!

Teach us, all, oh Lord to not give in to the enemies tricks!

But, to stand up, proclaiming victory, in the power of Your might!

For this, as Your predestinated children, is our divine right!

In Jesus' holy name, I pray, and for His sake!

Amen and Amen!!!

April 12, 2004 – Monday

Michelle Louise Pierre

WITH THE ENTRANCE OF EACH NEW DAWN

Genesis 1: 3 – 5
And God said, Let there be light: and there was light.
And God saw the light, that it was good: and God
divided the light from the darkness. And God
called the light Day, and the darkness he called Night.
And the evening and the morning were the first day.

Whomever you are, I know you will be
the man for whom my heart will beat.
The LORD has promised me that you are the
one to whom I can go, to find safety and retreat.

You will be the one, whose arms are big and
strong enough, to soothe away all pain.
The one, whose love I will be blessed
to receive, in Jesus' holy name.

My Darling Heart, you and I were definitely
fashioned for each other, being Spirit led.
You and I, will have both been reborn,
by the Spirit, in areas once left for dead.

Glory, hallelujah, sweet Holy LORD, Most High,
we thank You for designing us for one another!
Thank You, Father God, for birthing in our very souls
the burning desire to love, second only to You, each other.

Continue to teach us how to cleave to one another, after we meet,
as this time of purification, preparation and pruning presses on.
Then, when our wedding day does come, we will be able to love each
other, freely and uninhibited, with the entrance of each new dawn.

July 18, 2006 – Tuesday

In A Solitary Way

WITHIN ...

Song of Solomon 7: 10 – 13
I am my beloved's, and his desire is toward me. Come, my beloved, let us go forth into the field; let us lodge in the villages. Let us get up early to the vineyards; let us see if the vine flourish, whether the tender grape appear, and the pomegranates bud forth: there will I give thee my loves.
The mandrakes give a smell, and at our gates are all manner of pleasant fruits, new and old, which I have laid up for thee, O my beloved.

Dear Lord, within his eyes,
I will truly have found the love
that will set my heart at peace.
Within his arms, I will be able
to rest in a way that will bring
about the sweetest release.

Within my eyes, he will see
the reality of a love that was only
dreamed about, but not ever known.
Within my arms, he will find
a restful place that will bring
contentment right down to the bone.

Within Your eyes, we appear as Your
children, covered in the blood of Your Son,
Jesus the Christ, set free and twice born.
Within Your arms, we find forgiveness,
and the desire to live lives that raise
the standard, now, in royal robes adorned.

Within the circle of the Holy Spirit, we will
be able to maintain the standard of holiness,
that You are calling us to meet.
Within the shadow of Your wings, we will
be able to fellowship together in a godly manner,
as one, actively pursuing victory, not defeat.

July 18, 2006 – Tuesday

Michelle Louise Pierre

WITHOUT A DOUBT

Without a doubt, I will hold on
to all that You, Dear LORD, have
shown me in our solitary times, alone.
I will not turn back to using fleshly methods,
that ultimately sucked the life out of me,
leaving me feeling dry as a bone.

But, like those dry, dead bones in the
Old Testament, I, too, must heed
Your command to get up and live!
For, You have certainly done way too much
for this single heart, even when I have been
ungrateful for the things You graciously did give.

LORD, thank You, for never giving up on me
and giving me what I truly deserved, because
of my willful disobedience to Your command.
Father God, thank You, for Your faithful love,
wrapped securely around my heart, teaching me
how on Jesus' blood to be covered, and to stand.

Glory to God in the highest, as from my
belly living water is flowing freely, again,
while giving You, Your due, I give a shout.
For, I am truly blessed indeed with
the sweet assurance that my hope must
squarely remain in You, without a doubt.

Ezekiel 37: 3 – 6
And he said unto me, Son of man, can these bones live? And I answered,
O Lord GOD, thou knowest. Again he said unto me, Prophesy upon these bones,
and say unto them, O ye dry bones, hear the word of the LORD. Thus saith the Lord
GOD unto these bones; Behold, I will cause breath to enter into you, and ye shall live:
And I will lay sinews upon you, and will bring up flesh upon you, and cover you with skin,
and put breath in you, and ye shall live; and ye shall know that I am the LORD.

October 10, 2006 – Saturday

In A Solitary Way

<u>WRITTEN IN HEAVEN</u>

Romans 8: 26 - 31
Likewise the Spirit also helpeth our infirmities: for we know not
what we should pray for as we ought: but the Spirit itself maketh intercession
for us with groanings which cannot be uttered. And he that searcheth the hearts
knoweth what is the mind of the Spirit, because he maketh intercession for the saints
according to the will of God. And we know that all things work together for
good to them that love God, to them who are the called according to his purpose.
For whom he did foreknow, he also did predestinate to be conformed to the image
of his Son, that he might be the firstborn among many brethren. Moreover whom
he did predestinate, them he also called: and whom he called, them he also justified:
and whom he justified, them he also glorified. What shall we then say to these things?
If God be for us, who can be against us?

We are the baby boy and girl, who were born
miles apart, with separate lives, growing
up without any knowledge of each other,
as day grew into night, time and time, again.
Only You, our wonderful Savior, are due our
sincerest thanks, coupled with glory and honor,
for orchestrating this divine appointment,
our sweet Intercessor and Beloved Friend!

LORD, we know that only Your hand could have
so finely weaved and prodded us to the place
where we would seek out each other, and fall into
a love that neither of us, thought even existed.
Thank You, LORD, for being with us now, individually,
and for pouring Your divine love upon us, as we
desire to give our will over to You; so, we
may live, as You, in Your Word, have insisted.

Then, that human love will grow stronger, daily
intertwined with Yours, as You settle within our
hearts the desire to work towards, one day, cleaving
to each other in faith, coupled with passionate feeling.
For, we know You, alone, will successfully guide
us in the ways of sustaining this preordained,
covenant marriage, that will keep our love alive,
over the years, in ways both, humorous and thrilling.

Father God, help us to remain faithful to the
path You've placed us on, when we get to know each
other, and begin working out those things necessary
to make our future marriage a predestined success.
Help us not to wander off right or left, but to
stay on course, to be there for one another,
in sickness and health, when the money flows and
when it trickles, without doubting or undue stress.

Thank You, for birthing inside of us the desire
and the need for one another, as only You can;
for, without You, we know that we would just be
shipwrecked with others, and miserable once again.
Dear LORD, blessed be Your holy name,
for moving in grace, mercifully turning our
hearts back to You, and away from the paths of
destruction we trudged on, unstable from within.

Thank You, LORD, for healing our inner man,
so that when this love presented itself, we could see
through the eyes, of minds that had been renewed,
from spending time dedicated solely to You.
Build our foundation solidly upon The Rock, Jesus,
our Savior and LORD, who left us the precious
gift of the Holy Spirit, who leads and guides us,
while residing in our souls, all our lives through.

Without this divine assistance, we know that we
could do no good thing and would only ruin
what You had preordained to glorify You,
while in these tents, of mere flesh and bone.
We accept the fact that no weapon formed against
us will prosper as we continue to pray and fast, while
leaning solidly on Your Word, fully assured that with this
three-fold cord in place, we never have to fight any battle alone.

July 12, 2004 – Monday

YET, AGAIN...

Colossians 1: 19 – 22
For it pleased the Father that in him should all fulness dwell; And, having made peace through the blood of his cross, by him to reconcile all things unto himself; by him, I say, whether they be things in earth, or things in heaven. And you, that were sometime alienated and enemies in your mind by wicked works, yet now hath he reconciled. In the body of his flesh through death, to present you holy and unblameable and unreproveable in his sight:

2 Timothy 2: 19 - 21
Nevertheless the foundation of God standeth sure, having this seal, The Lord knoweth them that are his. And, Let every one that nameth the name of Christ depart from iniquity. But in a great house there are not only vessels of gold and of silver, but also of wood and of earth; and some to honour, and some to dishonour. If a man therefore purge himself from these, he shall be a vessel unto honour, sanctified, and meet for the master's use, and prepared unto every good work.

Yet, again, will I praise Him as my
Savior and LORD, lover of my soul,
forgiver of my sins, and all things good.
Yet, again, will I desire that love
above all others, while sinking into
this faith walk, like I know I should.

Yet, again, will I strive to live a life
that brings glory to the name of
Jesus Christ, as my soul sings aloud.
Yet, again, will I hold my head up
and walk in victory, not as one
defeated, but as one Godly proud.

Yet, again, will I trust in the LORD,
who always works things out for
my good and His ultimate glory.
Yet, again, will I not allow intellect
to rob me of the deeply abiding joy,
that comes from living out His story.

Yet, again, will I say, "Yes!" to the
King of kings, surrendering my will to His,
in the time tested truth of humility, love and grace.
Yet, again, will I press towards the mark of
the high calling, so that I may one day, stand in His
presence, hear "well done", and behold His radiant face.

Yet, again, will I dive into His holy Word,
with the open heart of one, who has come
to know, for myself, that Jesus is real!
Yet, again, will I turn from the sin, that can come
up in a flash, like a beautiful glass glistening
on a dark shelf, to my divine destiny, steal.

Yet, again, will I not allow busyness to reign
supreme in my life, as a distraction to shake me
from this Godly foundation, upon which I stood.
Yet, again, will I voluntarily die to this flesh, settle
contentedly into this single life, becoming a living
testimony as a member of the royal priesthood.

Yet, again, will I sing the new songs of deliverance
You have placed within this well, once sick, soul,
once so stunted, as the result of misuse and abuse.
Yet, again, will I wholeheartedly surrender to Thee,
Father, Son and Holy Spirit, to be molded into
a vessel of honor, fit for the Master's use.

March 20, 2018 – Tuesday

In A Solitary Way

YIELD!

Proverbs 12: 11 & 12
He that tilleth his land shall be satisfied with bread: but he that
followeth vain persons is void of understanding. The wicked desireth
the net of evil men: but the root of the righteous yieldeth fruit.

Mark 4: 2, 3, 7 & 8
And he taught them many things by parables, and said unto them in his
doctrine, Hearken; Behold, there went out a sower to sow... And some fell
among thorns, and the thorns grew up, and choked it, and it yielded no fruit.
And other fell on good ground, and did yield fruit that sprang up and increased;
and brought forth, some thirty, and some sixty, and some an hundred.

Most often we see those yellow signs that say, "Yield" on
streets and some highway entrances, which most people seem
to totally ignore, barely turning their heads to check on the
flow of traffic, while at the same time, pressing down on
their accelerators, demonstrating very little caution or foresight.
Unlike that sign, the LORD, used the word, "yield" in these
two particular scriptures, one from the Old Testament
and one from the New Testament, to pose a thought
provoking challenge about what is being yielded from
these lives, that should be lived within God's holy light.

I remember many years ago, after I first got saved and a preacher read,
in our hearing, Mark 4: 1 – 8, my first response was, being a bit of
a high achiever, that I would not to be satisfied with a Christian life,
yielding only thirty or sixty percent; I wanted to be fully at
one hundred percent, completely sold out for the LORD!
Since that time, I felt that determination settle in my spirit, through all
of life's ups and downs; and, even though, I have not always lived up to
my end of the bargain, the LORD seems to nevertheless have taken me
seriously, put me in the press and the sifting process, while I learned to rely
fully on the Giver of these gifts and talents, on my own, I could ill afford.

• • • • •

Now, I was talking to a man the other day, who began to explain
some type of new age philosophy to me about death, that I patiently
listened too, out of respect; and, then very calmly explained to
him that I was a born-again Christian, who chose to believe
in what God says about life and eternity, in His Word.
He cocked his head back and immediately changed his tune by
saying, and I quote, "My religion is Christian, too"; then, he
began to back-peddle, in a very haphazard way, to come up with
some type of rationale for what he had just said, in the light of his
newly stated declaration, that would not sound too absurd.

I shared that as an illustration that being a Christian is more than just believing God is real, and maybe being able to quote a few scriptures or rote prayers, from childhood, while boldly standing up for everything, but Jesus; for, it is the outward lifestyle that demonstrates the inward manifestation, even in the face of life's challenges, because, to you, unshakably, Christ is truly now the LORD living within. Therefore, being a Christian is not about religion, but a relationship where the Holy Spirit is allowed, for He will not force compliance, to lead you in the way you should go, so that the fruit you yield, will not only be plentiful, but it will also have the sustaining power, in Jesus' holy name, to shine forth as purified gold, not brass or tin.

April 26, 2018 – Thursday
(From The Book – As For Me And My House)

In A Solitary Way

YIELD TO HIS PRAISE

2 Corinthians 6: 14 – 16
Be ye not unequally yoked together with unbelievers: for what fellowship
hath righteousness with unrighteousness? and what communion hath light with
darkness? And what concord hath Christ with Belial? or what part hath he that
believeth with an infidel? And what agreement hath the temple of God with idols?
for ye are the temple of the living God; as God hath said, I will dwell in them,
and walk in them; and I will be their God, and they shall be my people.

Bowed down, almost giving in to the weight
of decisions, made in the flesh, designed
to lead you away from the LORD.
You have committed yourself to someone,
who is trying to get you to compromise your faith,
because they are threatening to leave you, once more.

This has been the pattern of this relationship, almost
from the moment your eyes met briefly across that
crowded room; and, you, both, dared a second look.
Your heart began to beat so loudly when they smiled
at you, that all's you could think of was having
them in your life, no matter what it took.

Later, after the business meeting was over,
introductions were made by a mutual acquaintance
and you seemed to hit it off, right then and there.
You agreed to meet for coffee the next day and,
in the light of day, they looked so good to you,
you could only grin, nod and stare.

Somehow, in all that nodding and starring, you chose
not to find out if they were a Christian, because
that could wait for a later time, for sure.
They seemed like such a good person, how could they
not be saved; so, in the meantime, you could simply
get to know one another better, as a loneliness cure.

Well, that was months ago, now and needless to say,
they turned out to not want anything to do with the
LORD, but felt you should stay together anyway.
Now, you are so used to having them around, the idea
of "doing life" by yourself, again, causes a flood of
turmoil, anxiety and all kinds of emotional disarray.

So, here you sit, alone, trying to rationalize within your
mind, another compromise they say, in these modern times,
is needed to take your relationship to the next level.
You have not looked in your Bible in a long time because
it just hadn't felt right, plus you were way too busy; therefore,
those actions have failed to guard you from the wiles of the devil.

At that moment, a still, small voice began to call to remembrance
a time when you gave God all the praise, and did not make a
move, without consulting Him in prayer and His Word, first.
A long forgotten need, obscured by sin, began to build up
in your soul as the LORD continued to knock on the door of
your heart, the divine living water that would quench your thirst.

Once recognized, you fell to your knees, sought the LORD's
forgiveness in true repentance, born out of godly sorrow,
that set-off a longing, only Jesus' presence could fulfill.
As His love touched your heart, washing it clean, praise and
worship began to course through your soul, anew, calming
the storm, with the comforting words, "Peace be still".

You got off the floor, picked up the phone and placed that
call you had not wanted to have to make, to say that you were
choosing Jesus over them, for He had lifted the veil masking the haze.
Finally, firm in your resolve, shored up by the Holy Spirit, choices now
made in humble sincerity, while cleansed in Christ's righteousness,
you have allowed Him to reset your heart, as you yield to His praise.

March 28, 2018 – Wednesday

In A Solitary Way

YOU HAVE BLESSED MY HEART

Psalm 34: 1 – 9
I will bless the LORD at all times: his praise shall continually be in my mouth. My soul shall make her boast in the LORD: the humble shall hear thereof, and be glad. O magnify the LORD with me, and let us exalt his name together. I sought the LORD, and he heard me, and delivered me from all my fears. They looked unto him, and were lightened: and their faces were not ashamed. This poor man cried, and the LORD heard him, and saved him out of all his troubles. The angel of the LORD encampeth round about them that fear him, and delivereth them. O taste and see that the LORD is good: blessed is the man that trusteth in him. O fear the LORD, ye his saints: for there is no want to them that fear him.

Dear LORD, I just want to say, "Thank You!"
for You have thoroughly blessed my heart.
LORD, he has found me, at last, and just hearing his
voice on the telephone, brings Your peace in the inward part.

I am so grateful to You, LORD, for preserving our lives,
saving our souls, while maturing us as a woman and a man.
LORD, we, both desire to love and adore You, with all that is within,
and we are determined to walk according to Your divine plan.

We have prayed and waited, prayed and waited, many years, for each
other to come along; in fact, were actually on the verge of giving up.
Yet, You, in Your sovereign grace and mercy, kept strengthening us
to go on, each day, with a fresh oil anointing and an overflowing cup.

Blessed be Your holy name, sweet, magnificent LORD, God,
for You have shown Yourself, as usual, victorious and strong.
You have given us such an intimacy of love for You as single hearts,
that we can trust that our new love for each other, will also last eternity long.

Oh LORD, thank You, for giving me a man, whose heart
was already sold out, before I met him, completely to You!
LORD, thank You, for all that You have already done and for
all the hills and valleys, You will victoriously bring us through!

LORD, we desire to serve You, while adhering to the call that
You have placed on his, my, and our soon to be joined life.
We desire to be obedient, in holy faithful covenant with You, the
Divine Giver of all hope and love, hand in hand, as husband and wife.

In Jesus' name, seal this I pray,
as a covenant between us, this day.
Amen!

October 21, 2006 – Saturday

Michelle Louise Pierre

YOUR WILL, YOUR WAY

1 Thessalonians 4: 1 – 4
Furthermore then we beseech you, brethren, and exhort you by the Lord Jesus, that as ye have received of us how ye ought to walk and to please God, so ye would abound more and more. For ye know what commandments we gave you by the Lord Jesus. For this is the will of God, even your sanctification, that ye should abstain from fornication: That every one of you should know how to possess his vessel in sanctification and honour

Dear LORD, I know that my emotions, in the past, have gone on roller coaster rides that have left me feeling completely drained. Now, settled more in my spirit than ever before, I can nurture this peace within my heart that is like no other, since I gave You, full reign.

No, I have not given up all hope of one day meeting and marrying the righteous man, whom You promised would come to find me. I have merely stopped letting those thoughts consume so much of my valuable time, so that I can get back on track to my divine destiny.

Father, I know that I have walked, several times, through the valley of the shadow of death, and that, too, is a testimony that must be used for Your glory. For each time it has happened, Your rod and staff were right there to comfort me, keeping me alive, long enough to add page upon page to what is my story.

You have been Father, mother, brother, sister, friend and, most of all, the best husband any woman could ever hope to have, in this life. So, as I sit here now contemplating all that You have done for me, I have to question whether or not I really want a man in my life, with possible inherent strife.

If I never get married, again, I will also accept that as Your will for my life, and will merely continue to do all the other things, You have called me to do. Dear Jesus, Your will, is that I do what our Father has in mind, to bring more souls into the Kingdom of God, by coming to, through the Holy Spirit, know You.

For it is only in this place of total surrender, that the possibility of never being married, one day, is a concept that I can warmly embrace, not hide from, or shun. Dear LORD, thank You, again, for bringing me to the place where I can say, and, mean it, albeit on bended knees with trembling lips, "Thy will, Thy way, be done".

October 23, 2006 – Monday

Michelle Louise Pierre

A

TIME

OF

REASONING

ISAIAH 1: 18 – 19

Come now, and let us reason together, saith the LORD:

though your sins be as scarlet, they shall be as white as snow; though they be red like crimson, they shall be as wool.

If ye be willing and obedient, ye shall eat the good of the land.

Michelle Louise Pierre

A GOOD THING

Proverbs 18: 22
Whoso findeth a wife findeth a good thing,
and obtaineth favour of the LORD.
(This is the only scripture, I could find, where a good
thing refers specifically to a person, outside of the Lord.)

1) Sisters, are you going to be the good thing that your man needs in his life? *(The good thing, I am finding, refers, more often, to the Word of God and His righteousness.)*
2) How much Word do you have in you, good thing?
3) Does His righteousness and righteous ways, flow through your soul?
4) Who's in charge of your spirit, anyway?

Deuteronomy 26: 11
And thou shalt rejoice in every good thing which the LORD
thy God hath given unto thee, and unto thine house...

1) Sisters, are you someone, whom your future spouse will be able to rejoice over?
2) Brothers, is this woman, whom you feel the Lord has given to you, for your future wife, someone to rejoice over spiritually?
3) Does she bring joy to your heart *(notice that the word was heart, not flesh)*?

Joshua 21: 45
There failed not ought of any good thing which the LORD
had spoken unto the house of Israel; all came to pass.

1) Has He promised you, your good thing?
2) Can you honestly say that you <u>really</u> know His voice?
3) Will you continue to wait patiently, allowing the Lord to prepare you, in all areas needed, until He gives you, your good thing?

Psalm 34: 10
The young lions do lack, and suffer hunger:
but they that seek the LORD shall not want any good thing.

1) If you are lacking and feeling hunger, could it possibly be due to the fact that you are acting out of the flesh as a means to satisfy your "appetites"?
2) Are you seeking the Lord to the extent that He desires to rain His blessings down upon you?
3) Are you in a position, in Him, to not only receive them, but to handle them correctly?
4) Can you truly be trusted with this blessing?

Psalm 84: 11
For the LORD God is a sun and shield:
the LORD will give grace and glory: no good thing
will he withhold from them that walk uprightly.

1) Are you allowing the Lord, to not only nourish you, but to protect you, as well?
2) Are you under the Lord's covering?
3) Are good things coming to you?
4) If you good thing is being withheld, are you walking uprightly?

Psalm 92: 1
It is a good thing to give thanks unto the LORD,
and to sing praises unto thy name, O most High:

1) Hey, good thing, are you thanking and praising the Lord?
2) Do you have songs that you sing to Him, the Lover of your soul?
3) Do thoughts of Him, cause your heart to sing?
4) Do you acknowledge His Lordship in your life?
5) Is He really exalted in His position there, twenty-four and seven?

Romans 7: 18
For I know that in me that is, in my flesh, dwelleth no good thing: for to will
is present with me; but how to perform that which is good I find not.

1) Are you allowing the Lord to cleanse and heal you, because you know that without Him, no good resides within you, as well?
2) Can you readily admit that you are not perfect, but are in need of the Holy Spirit's guidance as He moves you towards perfection?
3) Are you feeding your spirit daily on the dainties of the world, or on the Bible, which is the Word of God?
4) Do you confess your sins to God and ask for His forgiveness, as often as needed?
5) Are you willing to submit to authority and ask questions to gain additional insights into God's Word, when needed?

Galatians 4: 18
But it is good to be zealously affected always in a good thing,
and not only when I am present with you.

1) Can you, and do you, really, know how to, praise the Lord, when you are alone?
2) When it is just you and He, do you feel that you need to be in the midst of a crowd *(congregation, rally, praise service, etc.)* to go along with, or get into, the flow?
3) Does the Word of God cause your heart to stir, as your love for the Holy Spirit leads you to search it all the more?
4) Do you enjoy stimulating discussions *(whether as a participant or an observer)* centered around the Word of God, or do those type of situations make you feel uncomfortable?

Ephesians 6: 8
Knowing that whatsoever good thing any man doeth,
the same shall he receive of the Lord, whether he be bond or free.

1) What type of things have you been "dishing out" and then receiving right back?
2) Do you know that not having your "act together" by worldly standards, is no excuse for not having yourself together spiritually?
3) Have you lived long enough to discover, for yourself, that what you truly do sow, you will truly reap?

2 Timothy 1: 14
That good thing which was committed unto thee keep
by the Holy Ghost which dwelleth in us.

1) Has the Word of God found a place of commitment, within your heart, to safely reside in?
2) Do you allow the Holy Ghost to be the ultimate source of revelation to you?
3) Have you given the Lord permission to reign in your life and change your course, through the leanings of the Holy Spirit, whenever He determines the need?

Philemon 6
That the communication of thy faith may become effectual by
the acknowledging of every good thing which is in you in Christ Jesus.

1) What are you communicating to those around you?
2) What thoughts are allowed to roll around in your mind, day to day, moment by moment?
3) Do you have a testimony? *(A true story, of your own, about what the Lord has done for you)*
4) Can you effectively share with others, in some way, some of the good things that the Lord had done for, to, or through, you?

Hebrews 13: 9
Be not carried about with divers and strange doctrines.
For it is a good thing that the heart be established with grace;
not with meats, which have not profited them that have been occupied therein.

1) Is your heart established in grace?
2) Do you realize that your worthiness to receive eternal life is not predicated on your goodness, and that without God, you are nothing?
3) What type of things are you ingesting into your spirit?
4) Do worldly things rival the Lord's authority in your life?

Do you realize, the first good thing that you should actively pursue, is the heart of God
and His will for your life, now! Not after this or after that, but right now?

PRAYER

Sisters in Christ:
Dear Lord, make me a good thing, in all areas of my life.
Teach me how to keep my focus on You, as You draw him to me.
Cleanse, heal and restore me, according to Your divine will.
In Jesus' holy name, and for His sake, I pray. Amen.

Brothers in Christ:
Dear Lord, make my path straight and clear before my face.
Teach me how to be a godly man, who is worthy of her.
Cleanse, heal and restore me, according to Your divine.
In Jesus' holy name, and for His sake, I pray. Amen.

August 24, 1999 – Tuesday

Michelle Louise Pierre

A SONG

Song of Solomon 5:1
I am come into my garden, my sister, my spouse: I have gathered my myrrh
with my spice; I have eaten my honeycomb with my honey; I have drunk my
wine with my milk: eat, O friends; drink, yea, drink abundantly, O beloved.

1) He should not be trying to feed you from a place, where he has never been before?
2) What is he feeding on *(what kind of fruit is he consuming)* ?
1) What is he trying to get you to feed on, with him?
2) What has he cultivated in his garden?
3) What can, and what does, he cultivate in you, his future wife?
4) What do you, as a couple, have to offer to those who will come to you, to be fed?

As most of us already know, the book in the Bible, <u>Song of Solomon</u>, is considered one of the most poignant descriptors of the love that God has for his church, depicted by the love of a man for his wife, and a woman for her husband. As I sat there, during my devotional time, asking the Lord why He had chosen to lead me to this book, again, and this scripture in particular, He led me deeper into it than I had gone before. He gave me the above questions to meditate upon and it changed my viewpoint, dramatically. For those of us, who have not been called to be single, for the remainder of our years left on this earth, these questions should be rolling around in your mind, when you feel led to take a Christian friendship to the "next level", whether you are male or female. Spiritual discernment is always needed. We should, all, ask ourselves the following questions, and make them personal.

1) Am I trying to feed someone from a place *(of holiness and righteousness)* that I have never been to before?
2) What am I feeding on? What kind of fruit am I consuming?
3) What am I trying to get him/her to feed on, with me?
4) What exactly is in my garden *(weeds need to be rooted out)*? What am I cultivating? *(Would I actually know a weed, before it wrapped around my neck and tried to choke the life out of me?)*
5) What can, and what do, I cultivate in you, my future spouse? *(Are you, or they, better, for the relationship or worse? Is Christ in the center or off to the side, somewhere, like a referee waiting to be called in, only in times of heated dispute?)*
6) Are my ministry gifts and talents compatible with yours, so that when the Lord sends those in need to us, we feed them out of a cup of harmony and not strife?

PRAYER

Dear Father, help me to cultivate a garden that is full of Your goodness, today. Help me to discern the wheat from the tares; and, to handle them according to Your Word.
In Jesus' name, I pray. Amen.

June 22, 1999 – Tuesday

IF THINE EYE BE SINGLE

MATTHEW 6: 22
The light of the body is the eye: if therefore thine eye be single,
thy whole body shall be full of light.

LUKE 11: 34
The light of the body is the eye: therefore when thine eye
is single, thy whole body also is full of light; but when
thine eye is evil, thy body also is full of darkness.

As single adults, we sometimes have a tendency to scatter our energies to the four winds, in our attempts to serve God, with all that is within us. After all, we are told often enough, either verbally or subtly, that because we are single, especially if we do not have children yet, that that is what we are supposed to do. So, we end up signing up, or allowing ourselves to be signed up, to aid and assist in as many ministries as we have the waking hours to pursue. In the long run, we end up finding ourselves, dropping the ball all over the place, as we struggle to maintain some semblance of a servant's attitude of unconditional love, humility and graciousness. This becomes increasingly more difficult, as time goes on, because in all of the ministering that we are doing, we are not, ourselves, taking the time to be ministered too. It is interesting, and I have fallen prey to this myself, that in all of the busyness, the Lord starts to gradually take a backseat to our expectations, as well as the expectations that we have allowed others to place upon us. We begin, as our focus starts to gradually shift, to be more concerned with what someone else is thinking about our "service", than we are as to whether or not Christ is truly being glorified. It is a very subtle trap and the enemy of our soul, uses it very effectively, time and time, again.

In keeping our single focus, we must remember the One, who gives us life and salvation, over and above, all else. No, we are not to become selfish, in our pursuit of Him, to the extent, where you are, as they say, "Heaven bound, but no earthly good". But, we are to establish a routine of daily prayer, Bible study and devotion to the Lord. The length of time that this will take, depends solely upon you, and your personal relationship with Jesus. I, myself, started out with five minutes, first thing in the morning, at the initial stages of my walk. Looking back on that now, I remember finding myself looking at the clock, every minute, wondering when the five minutes would be up *(smile)*. I can only thank the Lord, that He helped me to remain focused enough to get to the point, where now time is no option. Yes, I do have a lot of things on my plate, as well, but when I think about what I went through the last time, that I decided man was more important than God, I have learned to guard my time with Him, fiercely. That is where, being single, has some distinct advantages, amongst others. I do not have to have a "prayer closest" per se, because my home is my prayer closet.

May we always remember that the Lord desires a personal relationship with us, over and above, anything else that we could do in His name. After all, the time that we spend with Him, will show up in our eyes, anyway. Let's keep them full of His light!

Is Your Eye Single?

1) What do you focus most of your time and energy on? *(Write it down and look at a schedule of your day, your week, etc.)*
2) What, or who, causes the lights to go on in your eyes?
3) How much time do you spend vigorously pursuing relationships with man *(mankind)*?
4) Is fellowshipping with man, becoming more important to you, than spending time, alone, with God? *(Please, take time to do the math.)*
5) Do you find that you are too tired to pray or read your Bible, because of all of the needs that need to be met?
6) Do you find that the applause and "well dones" that you receive from man, are what really light up your life?
7) Are you determined to allow the Lord to reveal to you, areas in you, that need changing or purging, to the extent that waiting for "A Word" from man, takes a back seat to searching God's Word, for yourself; therefore, allowing Him the time necessary to speak a clear Word, directly to your heart?

PRAYER

Dear Lord, show me how, through Your Holy Spirit, to bring my Focus back to You, as I learn to pursue You, as I am pursued by You. Teach me how to keep my eye single, as I focus on those things that are pleasing in Your sight. I ask this of You, according to Your will, in Your Son, Jesus', holy name. Amen.

August 19, 1999 – Thursday

JUST DON'T LET IT TOUCH ME!

I remember sitting in church, last Sunday, feeling the waves of God's love pass over, and through, me. The congregation had just finished with a time of high praise and worship. Now, it was time for our pastor, Anthony Williams, actually "Pastor Tony" as we affectionately call him, to bring us a Word from the Lord. A calming hush had settled over the entire congregation, so that we could focus our full attention on the message that was getting ready to come forth. As he began to speak, something out of the ordinary came into view.

Please excuse me, but I must back up a little, to fill in a few details that led up to this new discovery. Previously, I had noticed that as someone had come to sit in front of me, before praise and worship began, they had casually brushed something away from their face. It looked, to me, like the kind of "creepy" reaction you automatically have when a spider's web touches your skin, especially your face. The moment I saw her reaction, it caused me to look up, and sure enough, I saw the remains of the tattered web, about eight feet above the sanctuary floor, hanging from the ceiling. Once noted, I put it out of my mind, not giving it another thought, as an atmosphere of praise and worship enveloped us. But, now, back in our seats, with our eyes focused on the pastor, I noticed that that web was not unoccupied, as I had previously thought it to be. Instead, it now had a small, tan colored spider using it as a mode of transportation, like it was on a down escalator in a crowded mall.

Needless to say, now that a few others noticed it, too, it was causing a minor disturbance. Still, at that point, only myself and a few others, on the second row, had become aware of its looming presence. I must confess that, from that point on, one eye and both ears were tuned into what the pastor had to say, but the other eye was definitely focused on that spider, as it methodically, inched its way down on that trail of remaining web. I knew that it was only a matter of time before it reached the "end of the line" and started a new one. As anybody knows, a spider can descend from point A to point B, a span of three feet or more in a matter of a split second. This continued for a few more seconds, then it seemed to realize its eminent demise and stopped. That's when Donna, our new church administrator, seated comfortably on the front row, whose husband had noticed it a few seconds before, noticed it for herself.

I could see the tension move into her shoulders as she slowly stared up at it. She was the closest "victim". It was not directly over her head, but even the slightest breeze would swing it her way. Still, it was several feet away. After the initial shock wore off, she leaned over to her husband and said in a hushed voice, "Just don't let it touch me!" Her husband gave her a slight nod of assent. Then she went back to devoting her whole attention to what the pastor was saying. As was inevitable, it finally dropped around four feet, causing us to gasp silently, and was swiftly knocked down by a fan in her husband's hand. After that, we all breathed an audible sigh of relief. Then the pastor said, "Thanks. That spider was interfering with my message." We, on the first two rows, all started laughing. The others in the congregation had no idea what was going on, and we had not even been aware of the fact that he had noticed it, too.

I have been pondering that incident in my brain, for the last few days. My first thought was, as a single woman, it would be nice to have so much confidence in my future mate that I could rest securely in his ability to look out for me, even when danger was looming overhead; all the while, knowing full well that he could handle the crisis. However, this morning, it fully hit me. Why was this so significant to me? Why was God bringing it back to my remembrance, over and over, again?

As the scene played back in my mind, one last time, I finally saw what my Father wanted me to see, and to know, all along. He wanted me to get beyond the natural and see with my spiritual eyes. He told me that through all of the dangers that have come my way, He has always been, and will always be, there to take care of me. He told me that He would in no way let anything harm me. He added that, if I ever became aware of a dangerous situation, or person, coming into my life, all that I would have to do is call on Him. Then, lean all the more completely on Him and He would take care of it, or them, for me. He finished speaking to my heart by saying that, I was to completely rest, in that fact.

Simple message really, but oh what peace it brought to my soul.

PRAYER

Father God, in the name of Jesus, teach me to always lean on You for direction and protection. Help me to remember that my fight is not in the natural, but in the spiritual. Help me to know that I must keep my faith and trust rooted and grounded in You, and I will always be all right! For truly, as You state in Your Word, no weapon formed against me, will ever prosper. In Jesus' holy name, I pray and give thanks!
Amen and Amen.

May 30, 1997 - Friday

ME, CAN DO IT!

If any of you have ever spent time in the presence of a child around three to four years old, the phrase, "Me, can do it!", said with just the right amount of pout and determination, should not be unfamiliar. Whether it is stated in the attempt to carry their own plate to the kitchen table, dress themselves, or secure their own seat belts "Thank You, very much", it is a phrase that can be heard from them, uttered several times throughout your busy day. As one, who is in charge of taking care of them, for that time and season, at first you just take over and ignore their little pleas of "me, me, me". This can actually go on for some time. Then, as you become slightly weary of always having to go through that "ritual", on a moment by moment basis, you come to the place where you decide to let them do it themselves, as you stand back and watch.

To your surprise, some of the things that "me" can do, amaze you in the success of their attempt. Still, in other areas, you know that "me" is in way over their cute, toddler heads, so you allow them the opportunity to make the attempt, which will ultimately fail due to their size and immaturity, while you stand in the ready to step in. When you do step in, you lovingly remind them that although there are things, now, that "me" can do, there are still others, that "I" can do better, because "I" am an adult and have lots of years of experience doing that particular thing. You might even add that you are doing it because you love them, and only want them to be safe. As the "me" becomes a little older, you add not only are you doing it because you want them to be safe, but you might further add the phrase "and not sorry", to the end. As "me" matures, more and more, you allow them to gracefully enter the "I" stage, and handle those things that they have been prepared to handle, because they have seen you demonstrate it to them, over and over.

As the Lord showed this to me, I felt like that is exactly how He must be with us. Here we are still in the "me" phase, in particular areas of our lives, but we don't want to listen to the "I", the great I AM, who will always be wiser and stronger than us, and whose ultimate desire is for our good. We don't want to wait. We want to, and do, in most cases, plunge right into the deep end of the pool, so to speak. Then, again and again, His loving hand of rescue is extended, right in the nick of time. Yes, there are things that we, even in the "me" stage of development can do; but, there are many, many others that we need to leave to the great I AM, to do on our behalf. Amen!

PRAYER

Dear Father, help me to know when I am in the "me" (toddler) phase and when I am in the "I" (adult) phase. When I am in the "me" phase, teach me how to lean even more fully on You, and allow You to take care of "me", as You deem best. When I am in the "I" phase, teach me to listen even more intently to the Holy Spirit, as "I" proceed on, in the confidence and maturity that "I" have allowed You to birth in my heart. Dear Lord, help me to never confuse the two, because they will forever be present within me. Thank You, Lord, for all that You have so lovingly, already done for me. I humbly ask this of You, in Jesus' holy and righteous name. Amen.

June 7, 2000 – Wednesday

STEP BY STEP

What a day - what a day! I have to back up to Monday, first, so bear with me, if you can. I was driving home Monday early evening, after teaching the last women's Bible Study series on the topic, "What Happens When Women Pray". The freeway was, as it is from time to time, totally backed up. As though that is not stressful enough, in of itself, the "Check Engine Light Soon" came blindingly on! That's when the negotiations began – let me get home, LORD, and I will take the truck to the shop. If you are like me, this is not one of our favorite things to do; in my case, not even when it is just for an oil change *(smile)*.

Well, today was the day. I had it all planned out. I would drive over to the mechanic, who is merely blocks away from where I live. Then, walk to my line dancing class, which is also blocks away from where I live, but in the other direction. After class, I would walk back home and then be ready to go out, again, near five o'clock *(because it is always ready about that time)*, walk back to the mechanic and pick up my truck. I have found that as a single woman, over the years, self-sufficiency and convenience, without having to rely on anyone else, or their schedule, is a high ticket item. It definitely helps to keep my stress level down. So far, all was running smoothly. When I called the mechanic back, after my class was over, he told me that I only needed a major tune-up. I praised God for that because the truck is eighteen years old, so that is indeed good news! That was actually going to be the end of my praise report. Hallelujah! But, after I picked it up, as I was driving out of the lot, I noticed my rearview mirror needed adjusting. So, of course, I proceeded to adjust it, and boom, it falls off, right then and there! *(I can laugh about it now – the next day. Then, I just made this sad sounding chuckle, accompanied with a groan. That groan emanated from the fact, that in all my planning, I failed to calculate the super, blazingly hot day it was destined to turn into. Therefore, when I was walking over there to pick up the truck, I found it was like walking in sand, to get my legs to move, again, after all that had previously gone on that day)*.

Now, get this, I was so happy to have my truck back, because in case you didn't realize it, when you are indoors, it may feel hot out there, but when you are walking around out there in that heat, all day, it can border on unbearable, for most native Californians. Still, the LORD helps you keep putting one foot in front of the other, even when having to wait for the light to change in the scorching sun, when instinctively you just want to run and find some shade. So, my new dilemma – do I simply go home, hot and tired as I am, and just hunt up some good old "gorilla glue" or "super glue"; or, do I just back-up, before exiting the lot, and see if my mechanic can do it for me. Being the independent woman of God, I am, it takes me a minute or two, to reason this out. Fortunately, God has been working on me about asking for help and that is okay to ask; so, I backed the truck up and asked for help. At first, he told me step by step, how to proceed and I listened intently. Then, he got it in his head, for some reason that it would be better if he just did it himself *(and, ladies – smile, I did not point out to him, that I was more than capable of doing it myself)*. However, he did not have the right glue on-hand, so I suggest that I could go across the street *(yes, across the street to the auto parts supply store)* pick it up, and bring it back. He agreed, and he would then take it from there.

Bear in mind, I had been praying for God to intervene, before I headed to the shop in the morning as well as when I was headed back there to pick up the truck. I did this because I am sure we have all had those nasty, little surprises that equate to much more money, after we get there, and the mechanic starts the song and dance, which goes something like this, "When I gave you that estimate earlier, I didn't realize that "a, b or c" would eventually need to be done, as well; so, you can either leave it with me, now, or bring it back in a couple of days, at the most" *(With a note of urgency thrown in, on the last phrase – as though, your vehicle will blow up or something if you fail to return)*. After I returned, he signaled me to come into one of the repair bays, ahead of another customer. I gave him the glue, he looked it over, I went to stand in the shade, off to the side and let him do his thing. When it was done, he gave me the signal to come over. Then, he reiterated that I needed to let the attached metal part set-in for at least twenty-four hours, before re-attaching the rearview mirror, which he walked me through, step by step. After all was said and done, when I asked him how much I owed him, for the extra labor, he said, "No charge". Then, he also apologized to me because he did not have the glue on hand, so I had to go across the street to pick it up myself.

As I drove off the lot, again, I realized that not only had he repaired the problem, but he had also, taken the time, while I was waiting, to clean my front window of all the debris that had accumulated on it. In fact, it was now crystal clear! Wow, what a nice guy! What a nice touch. Reflecting on it, now, reminds me of how the LORD, thinks about us, and does things for us, even down to the last detail. God, time and time, again, goes beyond what we expect, and always leaves us in a place, where our vision is much clearer than before. At times, when this happens, we don't realize at that precise moment, when the actual shift comes between confusion and clarity; but, as we know, we serve a God of order.

As I was re-editing this piece of work and "fleshing it out" a bit more *(I originally posted a somewhat shorter version of this, on a social media site's page for "Praise Reports" that was set up by my church, for I thought that was where this would end. But, when I woke up this morning, I felt prompted of the LORD, to add it to this book, before it was "officially" closed out)*, God spoke to me about all of the life lessons, He had been teaching me throughout that day.

I get it, LORD, and, as always, I am most thankful and grateful for Your divine interventions, even in what could seem to some to be a rather mundane day. I, however, choose to give You, all the praise, glory and honor that You are due! Thank You for being with me every step of the way.

So, in summary, in a roundabout way, what does happen when we pray? Simply answer – God happens, in whatever way He deems fit to do so. Thank the LORD for divine favor, yet, again! We most certainly do serve an awesome God!!! Praise the LORD!!! Hallelujah and Amen!!!

PRAYER

Father God, in the name of Jesus, continue to build within my heart the spirit of gratitude to the extent that I will give no one, or thing, credit for even the smallest things that You do in my life. Help me to always realize that when I pray, it is not to move Your hand in ways that I choose, but in the way that will be for my good and Your ultimate glory, as You fully intended it to be, from the start. Help me to pray for Your will to be done in my life, in all areas, big and small. Then, once answered, help me to accept Your will for my life, no matter what it looks like to the natural eye. In Jesus' holy name and for His sake, I pray. Hallelujah and Amen!!!

July 19, 2018 – Thursday – 11:01 am

PSALM 51

To the chief Musician, A Psalm of David, when Nathan the prophet came unto him, after he had gone in to Bathsheba.

Have mercy upon me, O God, according to thy lovingkindness: according unto the multitude of thy tender mercies blot out my transgressions. Wash me throughly from mine iniquity, and cleanse me from my sin. For I acknowledge my transgressions: and my sin is ever before me. Against thee, thee only, have I sinned, and done this evil in thy sight: that thou mightest be justified when thou speakest, and be clear when thou judgest. Behold, I was shapen in iniquity; and in sin did my mother conceive me. Behold, thou desirest truth in the inward parts: and in the hidden part thou shalt make me to know wisdom. Purge me with hyssop, and I shall be clean: wash me, and I shall be whiter than snow. Make me to hear joy and gladness; that the bones which thou hast broken may rejoice. Hide thy face from my sins, and blot out all mine iniquities. Create in me a clean heart, O God; and renew a right spirit within me. Cast me not away from thy presence; and take not thy holy spirit from me. Restore unto me the joy of thy salvation; and uphold me with thy free spirit. Then will I teach transgressors thy ways; and sinners shall be converted unto thee. Deliver me from bloodguiltiness, O God, thou God of my salvation: and my tongue shall sing aloud of thy righteousness. O Lord, open thou my lips; and my mouth shall shew forth thy praise. For thou desirest not sacrifice; else would I give it: thou delightest not in burnt offering. The sacrifices of God are a broken spirit: a broken and a contrite heart, O God, thou wilt not despise. Do good in thy good pleasure unto Zion: build thou the walls of Jerusalem. Then shalt thou be pleased with the sacrifices of righteousness, with burnt offering and whole burnt offering: then shall they offer bullocks upon thine altar.

On-going Prayer Requests

Father God, in the name of Jesus, Your precious Son, I thank You for forgiving me of my sins, those conscious and willful, as well as those unconscious and passive. Continue to strengthen me and lead me in the way, You would have me to go. Cover me under the blood of Jesus, with the anointing insured by the baptism of the Holy Spirit, Who reigns in my life! Thank You, for cleansing this vessel of dishonor and turning it into a vessel of honor, meat for the Master's use. I give You, all the praise, glory and honor, only You are due, as I humbly submit, again and again, to Your divine authority in my life.

Now, I lift up all singles, who call, and will call, You, Savior and LORD. I ask a special dispensation upon their souls, as they, too, navigate, through this world, with their minds, bodies and hearts in intimate relationship, and fellowship, with You. Give them, the clarity and strength needed to remove themselves, from anyone, or anything, that would seek to unequally yoke themselves, or itself, to pull them off-course; and, away from Your throne, where they can receive the love, grace and mercy needed to continue to walk this earth, as Your holy witnesses. Cover them in the blood of Your Son, Jesus Christ, the Messiah, which, alone, has the power to wash away the stain of sin in their lives. Comfort them with the rich, abiding presence of the Holy Spirit in times when they, too, find themselves awakening in their own personal "pig pens"; as, they repent and obtain forgiveness, may they never, again, stray from under the loving shadow of Your divine protection.

I ask this all of You, Dear LORD, in the matchless name of Jesus, Your Only Begotten Son, and for His sake. Thank You, LORD!!! Hallelujah and Amen!!!

April 26, 2018 – Thursday – 10:56 am

IN CONCLUSION OF THIS MATTER

CONCLUSION – 2006

I have just finished reading the poetry section of the book and it has been like trekking through old areas of my life, and seeing them anew. I have also had memories rekindled of others, who touched my life in some way, during that time period. Thank You, LORD, for those memories. I am grateful for them, as well as for the ones that still lie ahead.

I had to smile, while reading these poems from A to Z, so to speak, because I could see that the path I walked on over those eleven years, certainly had its ups and down. Yet, as the old saying goes, "Hope springs eternal". I have not lost my zest for life, in the face of some rather crushing disappointments, but have chosen instead to engage myself, even more fully in embracing life for all of the good that the LORD has to offer.

I pray that you were blessed, to some significant degree, by some of the things you read between the "Introduction" and the "Conclusion". If you are not saved *(In other words, you have not acknowledged the sin in your own life. Therefore, you do not realize the need for the Savior, Jesus Christ, to forgive you of sins.)*, my prayer is that you, too, will desire to come to know Him for yourself. For those, who are saved, and know it with a certainty that only you can, I pray that you, too, will be moved to step out on faith and do what the LORD has called you to do. Only you know what that is, and only He can show you how to do it. I pray that every single person, who reads these words, will be encouraged in some way, to continue to walk in your season of singleness, head held up high, with anticipation engrained in every step. Do not lose heart and stay encouraged. Consider the words in this book, as a plate of food set before you. Eat what the LORD leads you to eat to nourish your soul, and leave the rest. Leftovers are better, after all.

In conclusion, a lot of life has been lived between the words that fill these pages, some good and some not, some honorable and some dishonorable. I simply have learned to be thankful to the LORD for His patience with me, as I have walked most of my adult life, as a single person *(I was married from August of 1982 to December of 1985)*. I thank You, Father God, for Your love, grace and mercy. I thank Jesus, for Your sacrificial love, which atoned for my sins. I thank the Holy Spirit, for Your comfort, the wisdom and understanding that had led me to know even more about my heavenly Father and Savior. More than anything, I pray that I have been faithful, and will remain so, to the call that the LORD has on my life. To God be the glory! Amen and Amen!

Loving Him All The More,
Michelle Louise Pierre

November 11, 2006
Saturday – 4:51 PM

21stcenturypsalmist@gmail.com
www.21stcenturypsalmist.com

AN UNCOUPLED SOUL, IN THE MIDST OF MOURNING

I sit here in front of my computer attempting to gather my thoughts for this final commentary in the closing of this book, "In A Solitary Way". As stated in the introduction, I had originally planned to publish this work in 2006. However, life happened, and it ended up on the back shelf, until the end of 2017. Since such a long time had gone on between the first poem included, and that "dust off" date, I felt prompted of the LORD to add a few more poems. At the time, I had no idea what "a few" meant. I have now found out that He meant quite a few more, than was my original intent. During the same time, I was putting the finishing touches on my first published work, "While I Have My Being", to update it as a second edition; thereby, making it available in this modern time as an e-book, as well. I wrote all that, to state that I felt my life was on an even keel, and in a short period of time, I would have completely updated this book and be on to the next one, which is actually the first one that I ever completed, "Altars of Praise, Worship, Healing and Deliverance", also going to soon be getting a trip off that shelf. If you have not guessed it by now, I have several more books on that same shelf. I will be praying as to the order the LORD wants me to release each one, while at the same time, continuing to work on the ones that are not yet complete. We serve an amazingly awesome God!!!

Now, back to the now, and here I sit. Ready, set, go! Bam! All my plans were put on hold, when on April 2nd, I was informed that my mother, Mary Louise Wright-Pierre, aged 88, had passed away. It was not sudden, or even unexpected, but it still felt like I was frozen in time. I just stood there with my cell phone in my hand, as I let that information process through my soul. After initially processing the information and feeling like I wanted to get dressed and rush back out onto the necessary freeways to my family's side, the LORD reminded me that I still had two things on my plate for that day *(As in most other cases, death is not convenient, nor, hopefully, will it ever be)*. One, I was supposed to be teaching a women's Bible study in less than three hours; and, two, I was also on the "wait and see" list to possibly have to report to jury duty that same afternoon! As I stood there in the kitchen, having just taken my phone off the charger, I tried to come up with a way that I could go to San Jose, call in at 11:30 and get back to Oakland, if necessary, for jury duty. Because of the possibility of jury duty, I had already asked another sister to teach in my stead *(Thank you, Linda Lake, for your "Yes" without hesitation)*. However, I had already told her, the previous evening, it would no longer be necessary. Still, I knew, I would only need to let her know that I needed her to step-in, and that would have been settled. So, in the midst of my jumbled thoughts, and visions of me fighting traffic, over several freeways to get back to Oakland, while maintaining my cool, the LORD called it all to a halt, with these few words, "This is when faith meets the fire". I immediately took a deep, calming breath and prayed, "What do You want me to do, LORD?" Then, I saw that my family would be okay, and that I would be teaching that Bible study in San Lorenzo, after all. As the study came to a close, I would make the necessary call to check in on jury duty. If I would not be needed, I would then head down to San Jose. Once that decision was made and I let my family know what I would be doing, I could take that much needed breath. Still, standing in the same spot *(I just realized that I never moved that entire time)*, I saw myself struggling with the ability to go get dressed, in order to leave my home, to teach a Bible study, in the near crippling light of this fresh loss.

Then, I felt the LORD speak these words to me, over and over, "When faith meets the fire". In the process of the way the LORD prompts me to write, I often hear "titles/themes" played over in my head, again and again; so, I knew I needed to get to my keyboard and write, as He led. That is how that poem was birthed within an hour or so, of my first hearing the news. I finished it, and texted my pastors to let them know what had happened. I also let them know that I would still be teaching and that God had also given me a poem, along with its title. Long story, made somewhat shorter – as I taught the Bible study, I felt the anointing of God, as never before, shoring me up. I felt the undeniable presence of the Holy Spirit bringing comfort to my soul. I felt the prayers of the saints as their loved poured over me. I felt it all and I was blessed to be used to teach/minister the Word of God, in due season. I remember one of my Christian sisters, who was also present at the study, asking me in an excited voice, after she found out that my mother had just passed away, "My God! Why are you here!?" To me, the answer was simple, "As a Christian, who has been called to teach the Word of God, this relationship has to be real or I may as well pack it all in, go party, get a man, and get drunk". You see, faith must be an active, breathing thing, full of the life of the Creator. If it is merely flat words on a page or verses memorized in Sunday school, then there really is no true substance, no grace, no love, no peace, no contentment, no comfort, no real, unspeakable joy, that can only be found in an intimate relationship with the LORD! I found out that day, in a way, far beyond any that had come before, that to me, my faith in the finished work of Calvary, through the shedding of the blood of Jesus Christ, the Messiah, is indeed real! My faith in the power of the Holy Spirit to be my Comforter and Teacher, is indeed real! My faith in the omniscient, omnipotent, omnipresent Father God to put this all in place for my good, and His glory, before the foundation of the world, is indeed real!

Over the course, of the time that led up to the actual memorial service, the following week, I found that when I felt like just letting my soul cave-in, a fresh wind would blow over me, and I could again hold up my head and press on. Most people only see the outward calm, but not the inner struggle that wars within the soul of a believer, determined to stand in the power of God's might and be His witness.

Through it all, my dear fellow, Christian singles, I never once felt sorry for myself or felt that I would have been able to go through this "more easily" if I had a mate. In fact, it was not until, I was heading home in my truck, after a "goodbye lunch" with my oldest sister and her oldest son, my nephew, Mark, who would be headed back to Arkansas, later that day, as well as with most of my other immediate family members, that that fact came to me. In all honesty, it caught me by surprise! God also showed me something else. It is better to go through this with Him, alone, than with a mate, who might be unable to understand the depth of your pain, or the depth of your faith. For, these are truly the type of times that can, try the soul.

I look around me now, feeling whole, still with the confidence that my Godly mate is out there. I know that when the LORD has completely prepared our hearts, and we are equally yoked, we will meet; and, it will indeed be for our good, but more apropos, for His glory!!! Hallelujah and Amen!!!

In Love With The Creator
In Love With The LORD
In Love With The Comforter Of All

April 24, 2018 – Tuesday – 3:50 pm

CONCLUSION – 2018

What can I say, other than the fact that in finally putting the final touches on this work, this labor of love, the LORD has taken me to new places, higher heights and deeper depths in Him. It seems like with every delay, whether in years or months, and more so, even now, He has added a new layer to what I thought several times, over and over, was a completed cake. I have decided, like I should in all things, to fully acquiesce to the LORD's will, and allow Him to turn this project into a feast, not just an assortment of various meals.

In this process, even up to the last days, I have been brought back to certain poems, and felt the nudge to add a scripture and/or a rewording that fit just right. God, You are most definitely awesome! While also looking back, I unashamedly have to say, that I felt like tearing some of them up! Testifying to God's grace, mercy, favor and unconditional love, will not always leave you "in the best light", but it will serve to aid your brothers and sisters to come even further into His will, while surrendering what/who they thought they had to have, that superseded their affections for God! For as it states in *Revelation 12: 10 & 11*, *"And I heard a loud voice saying in heaven, Now is come salvation, and strength, and the kingdom of our God, and the power of his Christ: for the accuser of our brethren is cast down, which accused them before our God day and night. And they overcame him by the blood of the Lamb, and by the word of their testimony; and they loved not their lives unto the death."* *In reading this scripture, I just realized that He prompted me to add it, today, 7.31.18, to what I felt was one of my most revealing poems, "When I Met Jesus, For The First Time".* Acquiescence under the leadership of the LORD is indeed a good thing, for in transparency, there is liberty!

Still, there are other times, in the editing process, while reading something over, I have felt tears of immense gratitude flood my eyes. I can never say enough times that the LORD has brought me a mighty long way. I will never cease to be grateful and humbled by the journey, we have been on together since my salvation date of July 7, 1984! I also cannot say, "Thank You" to the LORD enough times to cover all of the times before I was saved, where I gave credit to everything known to mankind *(intellect, money, ancestors, new age philosophy, youth, looks, physical stamina, education, etc.)*, for my ability to successfully, for the most part, maneuver through life. But God, You always remained faithful to this faithless heart, because You chose me before the foundation of this world, to be Your child. I would like to think that You knew, when I finally got a "real clue" and put my trust in You, I would come a place of submission to Your divine authority and, finally, do what You asked me to do!

I remember a period in my life back in 1992, where I had gone through a time when I felt bitterly betrayed by a man, whom I had been dating for quite some time. At that time, I had pretty much reached the end of my tether, and really felt like giving up. The LORD, instead came to my rescue, yet again, and gave me three scriptures that I quoted, or read daily, as my spiritual strength came back in full force. Thank You, LORD, for walking with me, moment by moment, through that dark, shadowy time, so I could live to see Your innate goodness, in the land in the living. Thank You, also for having me reach out to my youngest sister, Adrienne, who came at the drop of a hat, and talked "some sense into me". Little Sister, I have never forgotten that, and I never will.

Here we go, again, LORD, I thought that I was done with everything but the final editing and I wake up this morning, July 19, 2018, to hear You prompting me to make a few more additions to this book *(include the poem, "When An Intercessor Weeps" from a previous work, and expand on a social media post, I wrote yesterday, now entitled, "Step By Step")*, along with writing one more poem, which I am inspired to write after speaking to a new young lady at church this past Sunday named Kia Harris. She is in the final stages of completing her Master's Degree *(That one is entitled, "Steppin' Into The New")*. LORD, You are totally amazing! I humbly submit to Your authority as I stand in awe of Your greatness! Thank You!!!

In conclusion of this matter, I would like to say that this single season in my life lasted much longer than I ever thought it would, and it still, blessedly, continues. During this season, I have been able to be used by God to do things that He, foreknew, I would do more readily on my own. As previous stated, I have been divorced since 1985. It was during that separation period, before the final divorce, I cried out to Jesus, not just a nebulous/unknown/unnamed god, for the first time. I may not have really known what I was doing, but He did! I was answering His knock! Thank You, LORD!!!

July 27, 2018 – Friday
This book did not get finished, because it was not finished! God, in Your sovereign love, wisdom, grace and mercy, I thank You!!! 3:06 pm

I am sitting here, now, having just finished writing what could be, see I am learning LORD, that last poem to be entered into this book, "Conversations With Grace". The tears are forming because in completing it, a profound love washed over my soul. In times like those, I know it is the hand of God touching my heart, bringing comfort and peace to my soul, and those words will be used to minister to countless souls. What a mighty God, we serve. What a mighty God, indeed! 3:10 pm

I continue to add scriptures to more poems, as prompted by the Holy Spirit! 3:33 pm

July 30, 2018 – Monday
In this final stage of the editing process, I am coming across poems that were written over twenty years ago and, still they touch my heart in those secret places of fellowship that only the LORD and I share. Reading/reediting them gives me the unique perspective and seeing how far the LORD has brought me, while at the same time, feeling the joy of the newness of life that now surrounds my soul. I have had to stop and take short breaks along the way, simply to revel in the sweet touches that He has been extending to me, time and time, again, throughout this process. I stand in total awe of how the words come alive on the page in ways that can only come about under the anointing. I thank You, for that LORD. I thank You, for just being You! 11:42 pm

July 31, 2018 – Tuesday
Oh my goodness, I woke up this morning and heard the LORD tell me that today it was time to "seal this book". I was extremely overjoyed! Even up to today, more scriptures have been added, and one poem even received an entire new verse! I previously decided to jot down some running comments in this conclusion, since I was not really sure when this day would come, and I wanted to bring you along with me, as much as possible, through the process. For those of you, who also write, or feel inspired to do so, I hope this helps in a more intimate way, give you a view into the process. God knows where He desires us to begin and to end, as we use the gifts and talents He has given to us, for His glory. It is an ultimate blessing to be used by the LORD, on our individual journeys with Him. To all, I hope you found, within these pages, whatever you stood in need of, as the LORD used these words to minister to you, in some way. Thank you, for your support. If needed, I pray the Holy Spirit brings you into the knowledge you need that will set you totally free, in the name of Jesus! To God be the glory!!! Hallelujah and Amen!!!

Began: July 14, 2018 – Saturday – 3:12 pm
Completed: July 31, 2018 – Tuesday – 8:00 pm

Overwhelmed In His Love,
Michelle Louise Pierre

21stcenturypsalmist@gmail.com
www.21stcenturypsalmist.com

ABOUT THE AUTHOR

Michelle, a native San Franciscan and a born-again Christian, has authored several more books of poetry. She is a prolific writer, who took to heart, advice she was given, after having a non-fiction short story accepted by a magazine, years ago, then completely reedited it before publication, without her permission. The advice was simple, "Learn from the experience, copyright everything, and no matter what, keep writing." Whomever you are, who gave me that word of wisdom, all those years ago, I truly thank you!

Michelle currently resides in Hayward, California, with her 10 year old kitties, Buttons and Coco, littermates. She adopted them when they were nine and a half weeks old. They are a constant source of love, companionship and entertainment, all rolled into two; especially, when they are not cat-napping. She is a licensed Speech Therapist, who holds a B.A., C.R.S. Credential, and M.A. in Speech Pathology and Audiology from San Jose State University. She remains single with all the benefits that entails. Michelle is also now retired as a Speech Therapist from the Hayward Unified School District *(combined public service with East Side Union High School District, Cupertino Unified and Alum Rock Unified of over thirty years – during which, she worked with students from the ages of three to twenty-one)*. She enjoyed that season of her life and now is thoroughly embracing this new season *(Employed people often ask her how she feels about being retired. Her answer is a resounding, "I love it! It is great to do what you want to do, when you want to do it; and, if that means doing nothing at all, that is okay, too!" Those comments are usually followed by a very hearty laugh)*.

Some of Michelle's other interests include: reading, singing, playing her tambourine, dancing, sewing, crocheting, photography, wood working, playing around with technology, seeing new gadgets, obtaining knowledge, and gardening as well as teaching and ministering the Word of God to groups of fellow Christian singles, women, and within other small group settings. Michelle has overcome one of her long standing "fears", and discovered a passion for line dancing. She also recently went to her first blues festival and found that, to be a real treat, as well. Michelle is overjoyed that at this stage/season in her life, she is still making new friends, and sisters in Christ, who have proven to be real friends, indeed! God is faithful, and that is, indeed, a fact!

Closing Scripture
PSALM 68: 1 – 6a

But let the righteous be glad; let them rejoice before God: yea, let them exceedingly rejoice. Sing unto God, sing praises to his name: extol him that rideth upon the heavens by his name JAH, and rejoice before him. A father of the fatherless, and a judge of the widows, is God in his holy habitation. God setteth the solitary in families...

Notes and/or Insights

www.ingramcontent.com/pod-product-compliance
Lightning Source LLC
Chambersburg PA
CBHW080540170426
43195CB00016B/2630